MANDARIN CHINESE CHARACTERS MADE EASY

An Easy Step-by-Step Approach to Learn Chinese Characters (HSK Level 1)

ISBN: 978-1-951949-52-5

CONTENTS

1. Simple numbers! | 简单的数字!

2. How are you? | 你好吗?

3. What is your name? | 你叫什么名字?

4. Are you Chinese? | 你是中国人吗?

5. What date is it today? | 今天几号?

6. What time is it now? | 现在几点了?

7. I study Chinese! | 我学中文!

8. I love school! | 我爱学校！

9. There are six people in my family. | 我家有六口人。

10. Chinese Food is so yummy! | 中国菜太好吃了!

11. The weather today is very cold. | 今天天气很冷。

12. Where is the train station? | 火车站在哪儿?

13. Seeing a doctor! | 看医生!

14. My day! | 我的一天!

FREE BOOK REVEALS THE 6-STEP BLUEPRINT THAT TOOK STUDENTS FROM <u>LANGUAGE LEARNERS TO FLUENT IN 3 MONTHS</u>

✓ 6 Unbelievable Hacks that will accelerate your learning curve

✓ Mind Training: why memorizing vocabulary is easy

✓ One Hack to Rule Them All: This **secret nugget** will blow you away...

Head over to **LingoMastery.com/hacks** and claim your free book now!

CHINESE CHARACTERS HISTORY

Chinese characters, also called 汉字, are logograms developed for the writing of the Chinese language. First used in the late 2nd millennium BC, Chinese characters are the oldest continuously used writing system in the world. By number of users, it is the most widely adopted writing system in the world.

Some characters are inspirations simply drawn from the surrounding natures: the sun, the moon, the rivers and the mountains etc. They are usually stylized pictures of physical objects presented in horizontal, vertical or curved lines. Other characters, which are composed of more than one part, tell stories about how Chinese ancestors look at the world and their philosophy on life. The use of brush and ink started the long history of Chinese character calligraphy writing. Picasso, the world-famous painter, once said: "If I once lived in China, I would have become a calligrapher rather than a painter". Picasso loved Chinese writings and the representation, and he was very fascinated and curious about the old tradition of Chinese calligraphy.

The style of writing characters, however, has undergone a lot of changes over thousands of years of evolution, as illustrated below with the character for fish. Its current form at the bottom of the image is the simplified character, which has been used since the 1950s.

Oracle bone script
甲骨文 (jiǎ gǔ wén)
The Oracle bone script was used during the Shang or Yin Dynasty (c. 1400-1200 BC)

Bronze script
金文 (jīn wén)
The Bronze script was used during the Zhou Dynasty (c. 1100-256BC)

Large Seal script
大篆 (dà zhuàn)
The Large Seal script was used during the Zhou Dynasty (c. 1100-256BC)

Small Seal script
小篆 (xiǎo zhuàn)
The Small Seal script was used during the Qin Dynasty (221-207BC)

Clerial script
隶书 (lì shū)
The Clerial script and Regular Script first appeared during the Han Dynasty (207BC-220AD)

Regular script
楷书 (kǎi shū)
The Clerial script and Regular Script first appeared during the Han Dynasty (207BC-220AD)

Running script
行书 (xíng shū)
The Running script has been used for handwritten Chinese since the Han Dynasty.

Grass script
草书 (cǎo shū)
The Grass script is the Chinese equivalent of shortand and has been used since the Han Dynasty.

Simplified script
简体字 (jiǎntǐzi)
The simplified script has been used in the P.R.C since 1949. It is also used in Singapore.

There are around 55,000 Chinese characters in most of the Chinese character dictionaries. About 3,500 of them are relatively frequently used; among those there are only about 1,000 characters that are most used in every life.

Based on the way they are formed or derived, several different types of Chinese characters have been recognized. They are pictographic characters, indicative characters, ideative characters and semantic-phonetic compound characters. We will have a look at them in more detail.

PICTOGRAPHIC CHARACTERS - 象形字

There are about 600 pictographic characters. They are generally among the oldest characters. The few characters below date back to oracle bones from the 12th century BCE. Can you tell what they are?

Pictographs and their evolution	Character today	Pinyin	Meaning
	日	rì	Sun, day
	月	yuè	Moon, month
	山	shān	mountain
	水	shuǐ	water
	鸟	niǎo	bird

INDICATIVE CHARACTERS - 指事字

Indicative characters are a small category and contain characters that are direct iconic illustrations. Examples include 上 shàng "up" and 下 xià "down", originally a dot above and below a line.

上

shàng above

flipped upside down

下

xià below

IDEATIVE CHARACTERS - 会意字

Ideative characters are made of two or more of independent characters. The meaning of an ideative is usually derived from the meanings of its constituent characters. The first type of ideative characters consists of two or more of the same characters being combined to express the idea of multiplicity or quantity, as shown below:

Character 1	Character 2	Character 1+2
人 *rén* people	人 *rén* people	从 *cóng* follow
人 *rén* people	从 *cóng* follow	众 *zhòng* masses
木 *mù* tree	林 *lín* grove	森 *sēn* forest

The second type of ideative characters usually consists of two different characters used together to express an idea that combines the meanings of the constituent characters.

Character 1	Character 2	Character 1+2
人 rén person	木 mù tree	休 xiū rest
小 xiǎo small	土 tǔ soil	尘 chén dust
手 shǒu hand	目 mù eye	看 kàn look

Did you get the idea? We will look at one character together.

The character on the first row, 休, means to rest, it is made of a person on the left-hand side and a tree on the right-hand side. A person leans on a tree, that is rest, isn't it?

You might argue that the part on the left-hand side is not a person as person is written as 人 normally, but here it is written as 亻 in this character.

That is a very good question. We will introduce the concept of radical to help you understand.

One of the definitions of a Chinese radical or indexing component is a graphical component of a Chinese character under which the character is traditionally listed in a Chinese dictionary. 亻 is the radical representing people or person in Chinese language. People or person is written as 人, but when there are other parts joining 人 in a character, the 人 become 亻. This is particularly true when there is another part coming in from the right-hand side. One way to image it is to see it as 人 being pushed to the left.

SEMANTIC-PHONETIC COMPOUNDS - 形声字

A semantic-phonetic compound is also referred to as a pictophonetic compound. It usually consists of a semantic radical and a phonetic element. It is thought that more than 60% of all Chinese characters are constructed this way.

Semantic radicals can be independent characters or symbols. Semantic radicals indicate a semantic field, or what they are associated with. The phonetic element, sometimes an independent character on its own, provides certain clue as to the pronunciation of the compound. The below images show a few examples:

Semantic radical		Phonetic component		Semantic-phonetic compound	Meaning	Pinyin
氵	water	曷	hé	渴	thirsty	kě
口	mouth	曷	hé	喝	drink	hē
火	fire	少	shǎo	炒	stir-fry	chǎo

In some cases, the semantic or phonological connection in Chinese characters has become obscure, due to changes in character meaning or pronunciation over a long period of time.

PINYIN AND TONES

Until the middle of the last century, it was almost impossible for foreigners to learn the Chinese language. One of the obvious reasons is that Chinese characters usually represent concepts rather than sounds. There is no way to tell how a certain Chinese character will sound simply based on how it looks. In 1958, the Pinyin system was brought in and it is a Romanized alphabetical system used to indicate the pronunciation of Chinese characters. It is also called the Chinese phonetic alphabet. As its name suggests, Pinyin comes from the Roman alphabet, however it only has 25 out of the 26 letters of the Roman alphabet.

Chinese language is a tonal language. It has four different tones, which can be a headache for some new learners. The four tones are: 1st tone, 2nd tone, 3rd tone and 4th tone. They are also known as the high-level tone, high rising tone, low falling rising tone and a falling tone. Learners may have come across some characters that do not have any tonal marks and they are called natural tones.

RADICAL

Radicals play a very important role in compound characters. Learners can think of them as classifiers, so being able to recognize radicals helps in the learning, understanding and memorizing of new characters. Although there are traditionally 214 radicals, only around 40 to 50 are the most frequently used.

The table below lists a few frequently used radicals, their meanings and character examples.

Semantic radical	Meaning	Examples		
火	fire	炒	烧	烤
氵	water	渴	酒	汉
女	woman	姐	妈	妹
口	mouth	吧	吃	喝

The third radical in the above table is 女, which means woman or female. The character examples 姐, 妈, and 妹 all have this radical in them. They mean older sister, mother, and younger sister respectively.

CHINESE CHARACTERS STROKES

Chinese characters are made up of strokes, ranging from one stroke to several dozens. There are eight basic strokes and 16 derivative strokes. In this workbook we will be focusing on the eight basic strokes.

The table below demonstrates the eight basic strokes, their names, writing directions, and example characters.

Stroke	Name	Writing direction	Example Character
丶	Dot 点/ Diǎn	From top to bottom right or left	永
一	Horizontal stroke 横/ Héng	From left to right, the right end can be slightly up	十
丨	Vertical stroke 竖/ Shù	From top to bottom, normally straight	十
㇆	Bending stroke 折/ Zhé	From left to right horizontally and then vertically down, the ending of the vertical down can be slightly tilting towards the left side	学
㇀	Upward stroke 提/ Tí	Diagonal stroke from lower left to upper right	习
亅	Hook stroke 勾/ Gōu	Vertical stroke first and then a tiny rising tip at the end	到
丿	Downward-left stroke 撇/ Piě	Diagonal stroke from upper right to lower left	八
乀	Downward-right stroke 捺/ Nà	Diagonal stroke from upper left to lower right	八

STROKE ORDER AND RULES

Chinese character stroke order refers to the order in which the separate strokes that make up Chinese characters are written. Knowing the correct stroke order speeds up the memorization of characters and unlocks a deep understanding of the structure of the characters.

The stroke order rules are listed as below:

1) From top to bottom
2) From left to right
3) Horizontal stroke precedes vertical stroke
4) Middle stroke precedes strokes on left and right sides
5) Left-falling stroke precedes right-falling stroke
6) Enclosing strokes first, then followed by the enclosed strokes, finally the sealing strokes

The table below lists some example characters for each rule.

Rule	Example Character
From top to bottom	二, 三, 您
From left to right	火, 她, 他
Horizontal stroke precedes vertical stroke	也, 下, 工
Middle stroke precedes strokes on left and right sides	水, 小
Left-falling stroke precedes right-falling stroke	八, 人, 今
Enclosing strokes first, then followed by the enclosed strokes, finally the sealing strokes	四, 日

THE ART OF WRITING CHINESE CHARACTERS

The orders of the strokes are logical in a way. Many learners found that writing Chinese characters is very therapeutic. It has similar effects to human brains as drawing or painting. When we write the strokes, for example the vertical stroke, we start from the top and draw a line down. Is it coincidental how we write the vertical line conforms with how gravity works? Personally, I don't think so. This is the true beauty of writing Chinese characters. They are constructed based on the most profound universal laws.

In ancient times, Chinese calligraphy was regarded as one of four arts of the Chinese scholars. It is an art of turning Chinese characters into beautiful writing through pressure and speed variations of a pointed brush. The core principle of writing Chinese characters is balance. By following the rules of stroke formation and stroke orders, every character is displayed into a beautiful piece of visual art.

HOW TO USE THIS BOOK

All characters in this workbook are written in the simplified style. Today in Mainland China, this style is the official and only one in use. In Hong Kong and Taiwan, traditional Chinese characters are still in use. This workbook is written for new learners who have never learned how to write Chinese character before or learners who would like to take the HSK Level 1 exam. The requirements for the level 1 exam have been updated in 2020 to include more characters, this workbook reflects this updated change in the HSK level 1 exam.

By following the book and writing the characters step by step, you will find writing Chinese characters easy and fun. There are words and exercises at the end of each chapter for you to practice and check your progress.

Two indices are attached at the end of the book. The first one is an English Chinese index and the second one is the Pinyin index.

HOW TO GET THE AUDIO FILES

Some of the exercises throughout this book come with accompanying audio files.

You can download these audio files if you head over to

www.lingomastery.com/chinese-cc1-audio

SIMPLE NUMBERS! | 简单的数字!

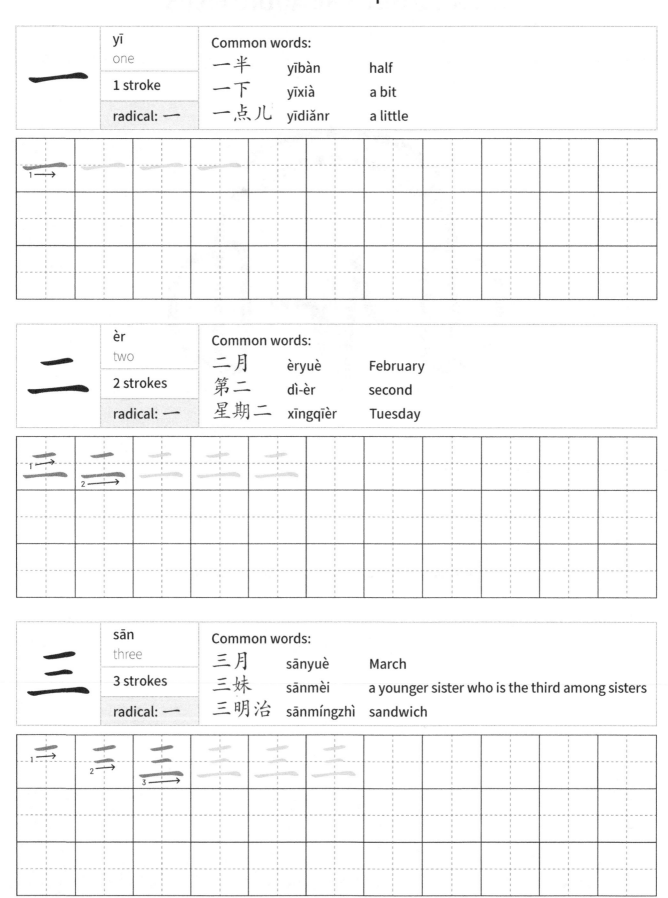

一	yī
	one
	1 stroke
	radical: 一

Common words:

一半	yībàn	half
一下	yīxià	a bit
一点儿	yīdiǎnr	a little

二	èr
	two
	2 strokes
	radical: 一

Common words:

二月	èryuè	February
第二	dì-èr	second
星期二	xīngqīèr	Tuesday

三	sān
	three
	3 strokes
	radical: 一

Common words:

三月	sānyuè	March
三妹	sānmèi	a younger sister who is the third among sisters
三明治	sānmíngzhì	sandwich

四	sì	Common words:		
	four	四弟	sìdì	a younger brother who is the fourth among brothers
	5 strokes	四季	sìjì	four seasons
	radical: 口	四处	sìchù	everywhere

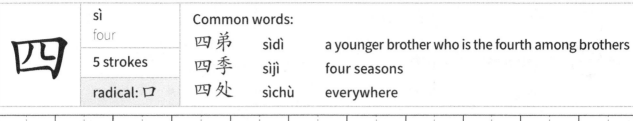

五	wǔ	Common words:		
	five	五岁	wǔsuì	five years old
	4 strokes	五月	wǔyuè	May
	radical: 一	五点	wǔdiǎn	five o'clock

六	liù	Common words:		
	six	六次	liùcì	six times
	4 strokes	六楼	liùlóu	the sixth floor
	radical: 亠	六个人	liùgèrén	six people

七	qī seven	Common words:		
	2 strokes	七号	qīhào	seventh of the month
	radical: 一	七楼	qīlóu	the seventh floor
		七百	qībǎi	seven hundred

一	七	七	七	七					

八	bā eight	Common words:		
	2 strokes	八十	bāshí	eighty
	radical: 八	八百	bābǎi	eight hundred
		八人	bārén	eight people

八	八	八	八	八					

九	jiǔ nine	Common words:		
	2 strokes	九号	jiǔhào	the 9th of the month
	radical: 丿	九月	jiǔyuè	September
		九百	jiǔbǎi	nine hundred

丿	九	九	九	九					

十	shí ten	Common words:		
	2 strokes	十月	shíyuè	October
	radical: 十	十全十美	shíquánshíměi	perfect
		十字路口	shízìlùkǒu	crossroads

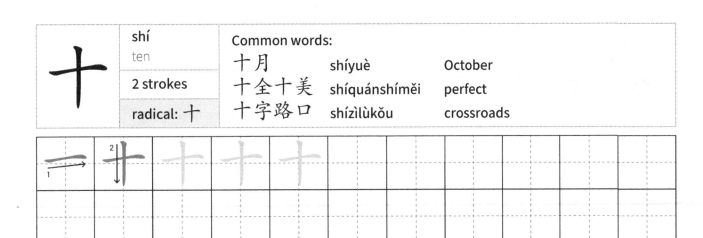

半	bàn half	Common words:		
	5 strokes	半年	bànnián	half year
	radical: 十	半天	bàntiān	half day
		三点半	sāndiǎnbàn	three-thirty (time)

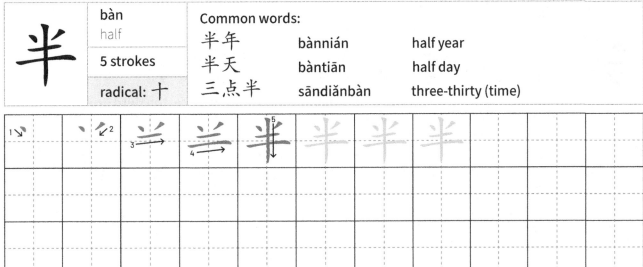

百	bǎi hundred	Common words:		
	6 strokes	一百	yībǎi	one hundred
	radical: 白	老百姓	lǎobǎixìng	ordinary people
		百岁老人	bǎisuì lǎorén	centenarian

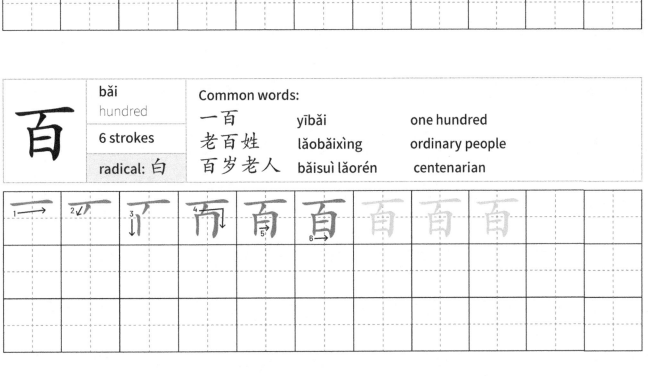

零	líng *zero* 13 strokes radical: 雨	Common words: 零钱　　　língqián　　　pocket money 零食　　　língshí　　　　snack 零时　　　língshí　　　　midnight, zero hour

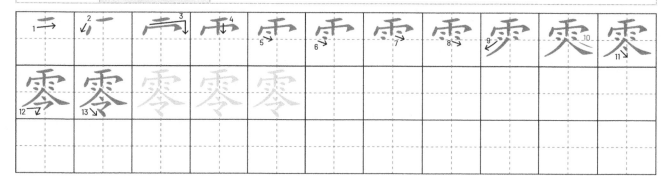

第	dì *prefix for ordinal number* 11 strokes radical: 竹	Common words: 第一　　　dì-yī　　　　the first 第一次　　dì-yī cì　　　the first time 第三名　　dì-sān míng　the third place, the third prize

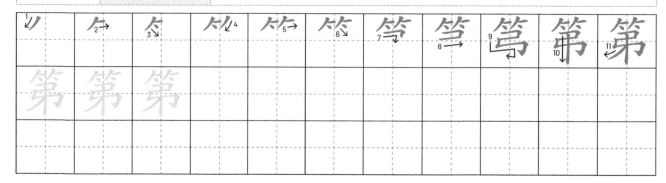

EXERCISE SET 1 练习一
SIMPLE NUMBERS! 简单的数字!

1. Write down the corresponding Chinese characters for the pinyin below.

(   )   (   )   (   )   (   )   (   )

    yī   èr   sān   sì   wǔ

(   )   (   )   (   )   (   )   (   )

    liù   qī   bā   jiǔ   shí

(   )   (   )   (   )   (   )

    bàn   bǎi   líng   dì

2. Listening practice: Number Game
Please listen to the audio and circle the numbers you have heard. See page 9 for audio.

0	1	2	3	4	5	6	7	8	9
10	11	12	13	14	15	16	17	18	19
20	21	22	23	24	25	26	27	28	29
30	31	32	33	34	35	36	37	38	39
40	41	42	43	44	45	46	47	48	49
50	51	52	53	54	55	56	57	58	59
60	61	62	63	64	65	66	67	68	69
70	71	72	73	74	75	76	77	78	79
80	81	82	83	84	85	86	87	88	89
90	91	92	93	94	95	96	97	98	99

3. Fill in the brackets with the correct Chinese characters.

(　　　)　　　(　　　)　　　(　　　)　　　(　　　)

zero　　　　hundred　　　three　　　twenty-two

(　　　)　　　(　　　)　　　(　　　)　　　(　　　)

half　　　forty-six　　seventy-eight　　nine

(　　　)　　　(　　　)

fifteen　　　fifty-seven

4. Please link each Chinese character with their corresponding pinyin and meaning in English.

三十二	wǔshíyī	seventy-nine
六十八	èrshísān	fifty-one
七十九	sìshísì	forty-four
十二	jiǔshíyī	twenty-three
五十一	shíbā	eighteen
四十四	qīshíjiǔ	eighty
八十	shíèr	thirty-two
十八	sānshíèr	ninety-one
九十一	liùshíbā	twelve
二十三	bāshí	sixty-eight

	wǒ	Common words:		
	I, me	我的	wǒ de	my
	7 strokes	我自己	wǒ zìjǐ	myself
	radical: 戈	我们	wǒmen	we

	nǐ	Common words:		
	you	你的	nǐ de	your
	7 strokes	你好	nǐhǎo	hello (to individual)
	radical: 亻	你们好	nǐmen hǎo	hello (to plural)

	nín	Common words:		
	you (polite form)	您好	nínhǎo	Hello!
	11 strokes	您早	nín zǎo	Good morning!
	radical: 心	您保重	nín bǎozhòng	You take care!

他	tā he, him	Common words:		
	5 strokes	他们	tāmen	they (male/male and female)
		他家	tā jiā	his home, his family
	radical: 亻	他人	tārén	other people

她	tā she, her	Common words:		
	6 strokes	她们	tāmen	they (female)
		她家	tā jiā	her home, her family
	radical: 女	她的	tā de	hers

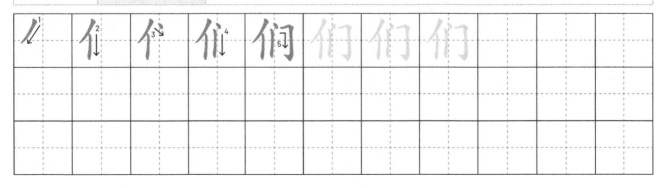

们	men plural suffix for human nouns	Common words:		
		我们	wǒmen	we
	5 strokes	老师们	lǎoshī men	teachers
	radical: 亻	同学们	tóngxué men	students

很	hěn very	Common words:		
	9 strokes	很好	hěnhǎo	very good
		很多	hěnduō	many, much
	radical: 彳	很远	hěnyuǎn	very far

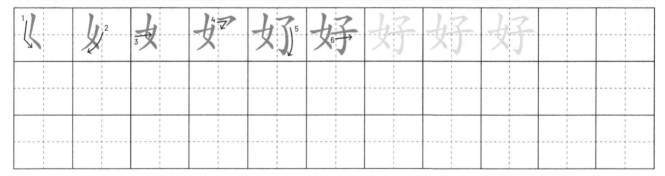

好	hǎo good, well	Common words:		
	6 strokes	好吃	hǎo chī	yummy, delicious
		好人	hǎo rén	good person
	radical: 女	好处	hǎochù	advantage, benefit

不	bù no, not	Common words:		
	4 strokes	不是	bù shì	no, not
		不客气	bù kèqi	you are welcome
	radical: 一	不对	bù duì	not correct, wrong

谢	xiè to thank	Common words:		
	12 strokes	谢谢	xièxie	thank you
		感谢	gǎnxiè	thank you
	radical: 讠	不用谢	bù yòng xiè	you are welcome

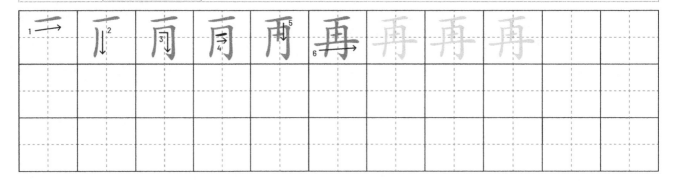

再	zài again	Common words:		
	6 strokes	再见	zàijiàn	bye, see you again
		再会	zàihuì	see you later
	radical: 一	再次	zàicì	one more time, once again

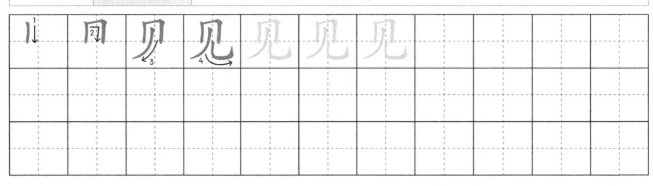

见	jiàn to see, to meet	Common words:		
	4 strokes	见面	jiànmiàn	to meet in person
		见老师	jiàn lǎoshī	to meet the teacher
	radical: 见	见家长	jiàn jiāzhǎng	to meet the parents

吗	ma	Common words:		
	question particle	是吗?	Shì ma	Is it?
	6 strokes	对吗?	Duì ma	Is it right?
	radical: 口	真的吗?	Zhēn de ma	Really?

口	口²	口₃	吗⁴	吗₅	吗⁶	吗	吗	吗		

呢	ne	Common words:		
	question particle	你呢?	Nǐ ne?	How about you?
	8 strokes	吃饭呢?	Chīfàn ne?	Eating?
	radical: 口	看电视呢?	Kàn diànshì ne?	Watching TV?

口¹	口²	口₃	吗⁴	呀₅	呢⁶	呢⁷	呢₈	呢	呢	呢

WORD PRACTICE

我们 **wǒmen** we, us

我	们								

你们 **nǐmen** you

你	们								

谢谢 **xièxie** thanks

谢	谢								

再见 **zàijiàn** bye-bye

再	见								

你呢? **Nǐ ne?** How about you?

你	呢								

EXERCISE SET 2 练习二
How are you? 你好吗?

1. Write down the corresponding Chinese characters in the brackets.

(   )   (   )   (   )   (   )   (   )

wǒ   nǐ   nín   tā (male)   tā (female)

(   )   (   )   (   )   (   )   (   )

hěn   hǎo   bù   men   xiè

(   )   (   )   (   )   (   )

zài   jiàn   ne   ma

2. Write down the following sentences in Chinese characters.

1) Nǐhǎo ma? Wǒ hěnhǎo, nǐ ne?

_____

2) Tāmen hěnhǎo, xièxiè, zàijiàn!

_____

3) Wǒmen bùhǎo. Nǐmen ne?

_____

3. Listening practice: Please listen to the audio and choose the words/sentences you have heard in each group. See page 9 for audio.

1) A. 谢谢!   B. 你好吗?   C. 你好!
2) A. 谢谢!   B. 你好吗?   C. 再见!
3) A. 你好吗?   B. 你好!   C. 他们很好。
4) A. 你好!   B. 他们很好   C. 我很好。
5) A. 她很好。   B. 你好吗?   C. 我们很好。

WHAT IS YOUR NAME? | 你叫什么名字?

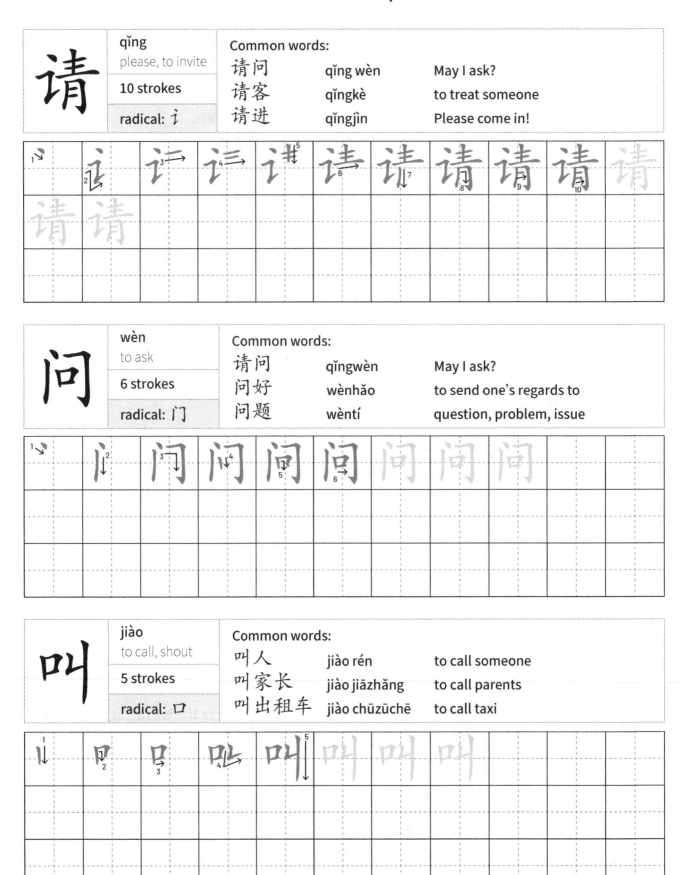

请

qǐng
please, to invite

10 strokes

radical: 讠

Common words:

请问	qǐng wèn	May I ask?
请客	qǐngkè	to treat someone
请进	qǐngjìn	Please come in!

问

wèn
to ask

6 strokes

radical: 门

Common words:

请问	qǐngwèn	May I ask?
问好	wènhǎo	to send one's regards to
问题	wèntí	question, problem, issue

叫

jiào
to call, shout

5 strokes

radical: 口

Common words:

叫人	jiào rén	to call someone
叫家长	jiào jiāzhǎng	to call parents
叫出租车	jiào chūzūchē	to call taxi

名	míng name	Common words:		
	6 strokes	名字	míng zi	name
	radical: 口	名人	míngrén	famous people
		有名	yǒumíng	famous

字	zì character, word	Common words:		
	6 strokes	汉字	hànzì	Chinese characters
	radical: 宀	写字	xiězì	to write characters
		字典	zìdiǎn	dictionary

什	shén what	Common words:		
	4 strokes	什么	shén me	what?
	radical: 亻	什么的	shénmede	things like that, and so on or etc
		什么饭	shénme fàn	what is for meal?

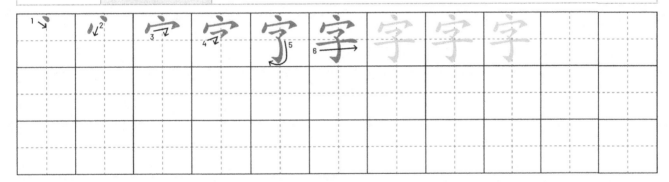

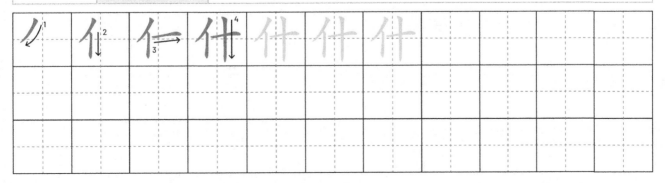

么	me	Common words:		
	interrogative particle	什么	shén me	What?
	3 strokes	好么	hǎome	Is it ok?
	radical: 丿	问什么	wèn shénme	to ask what?

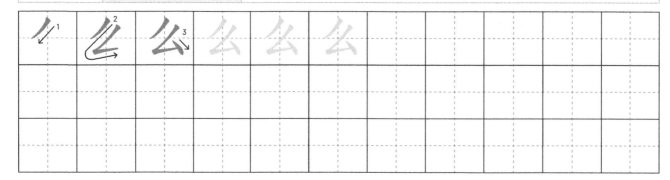

认	rèn	Common words:		
	to recognize	认识	rèn shi	to know, to meet, to recognize
	4 strokes	认为	rènwéi	to think
	radical: 讠	认真	rènzhēn	serious

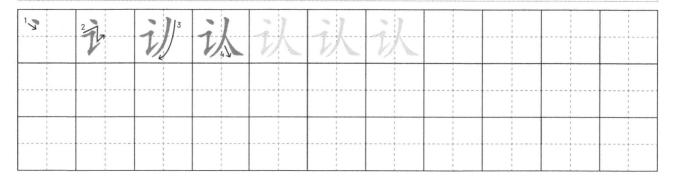

识	shí	Common words:		
	to know	认识	rèn shi	to know, to meet, to recognize
	7 strokes	识字	shí zì	to be able to read
	radical: 讠	见识	jiànshi	knowledge, experience

高

gāo
high, tall

10 strokes

radical: 亠

Common words:

高兴	gāoxìng	happy, joyful
很高	hěn gāo	very tall, very high
不高	bù gāo	not tall, not high

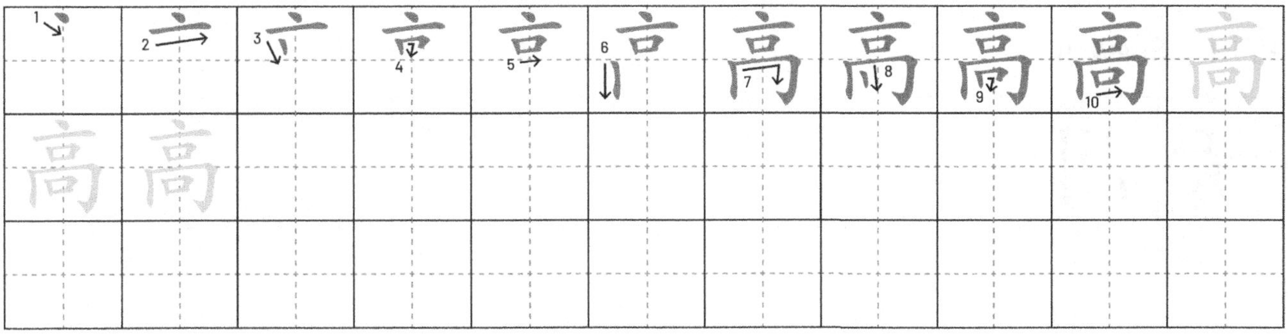

兴

xìng
mood

6 strokes

radical: 八

Common words:

高兴	gāoxìng	happy, joyful
兴趣	xìngqù	interest
兴致	xìngzhì	mood

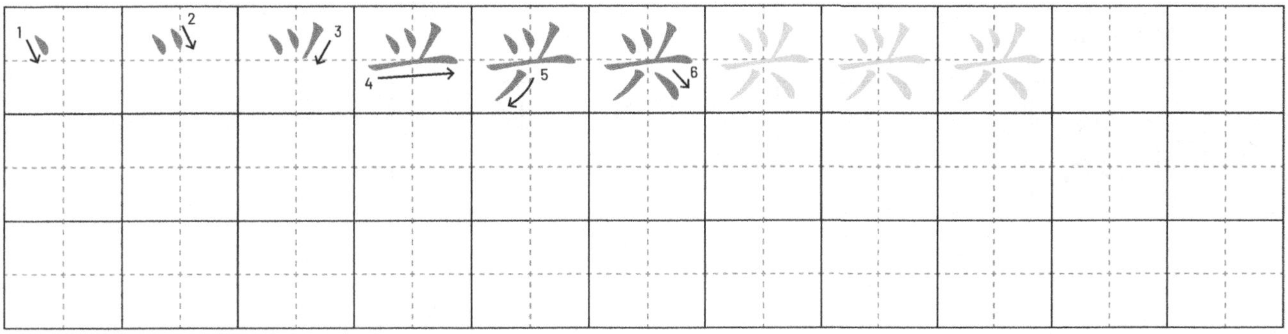

WORD PRACTICE

请问 **Qǐngwèn** May I ask...

请	问								

名字 **míng zi** name

名	字								

什么 **shén me** what

什	么								

认识 **rèn shi** to know

认	识								

高兴 **gāoxìng** happy

高	兴								

1. Write down the corresponding Chinese characters in the brackets.

(   )   (   )   (   )   (   )   (   )

qǐng   wèn   míng   zì   shén

(   )   (   )   (   )   (   )   (   )

me   rèn   shí   jiào   gāo

(   )

xìng

2. Choose the right character to make appropriate compound words.

wèn	míng	me	rèn	xìng
问	名	么	认	兴

请_____, 高_____, _____识, 什_____, _____字

3. Please translate the following sentences to Chinese.

1) How are you?

_____.

2) What is your name?

_____.

3) I am very happy to meet you.

_____

4) I don't know you.

_____

4. Please rearrange the words to form correct sentences.

1) 请问,叫你名字么什?

_____

2) 高兴很你识认。

_____

3) 们我认识你不。

_____

5. Listening practice: Please listen to the audio and choose the words/sentences you have heard in each group. See page 9 for audio.

1) A. 你好!　　　　B. 你好吗?　　　　C. 我不好!

2) A. 很高兴认识你!　　B. 认识你很高兴!　　C. 我不认识你!

3) A. 他叫什么名字?　　B. 你叫什么名字?　　C. 我叫什么名字?

4) A. 我不认识他(她).　　B. 她不认识我。　　C. 我不认识你。

ARE YOU CHINESE? | 你是中国人吗?

		Common words:		
是	shì to be, yes 9 strokes radical: 日	不是 是不是 是非	bùshì shì bùshì shìfēi	no, not yes or no right or wrong

		Common words:		
这	zhè/zhèi this 7 strokes radical: 辶	这儿 这里 这些	zhèr zhèlǐ zhèxiē	here here these

		Common words:		
那	nà/nèi that 6 strokes radical: 阝	那儿 那里 那些	nàr nàlǐ nàxiē	there there those

先	xiān	Common words:		
	first, prior, former	先生	xiān sheng	Mr., husband
	6 strokes	先...再...	xiān... zài......	first…then…
	radical: 儿	先后	xiānhòu	one after another, successively

生	shēng	Common words:		
	person, to be born	学生	xuéshēng	student
	5 strokes	生日	shēngrì	birthday
	radical: 丿	生命	shēngmìng	life

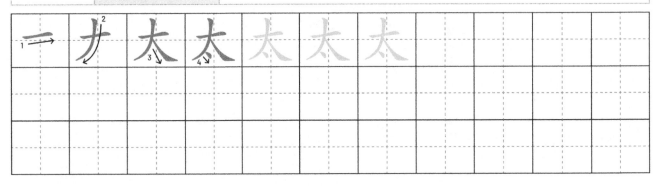

太	tài	Common words:		
	too, extremely	太太	tài tai	Mrs., wife
	4 strokes	太热了!	tài rè le	too hot
	radical: 大	不太好	bù tài hǎo	not very good

小	xiǎo small, little	Common words:		
	3 strokes	小姐	xiǎojiě	Miss
	radical: 小	小孩儿	xiǎoháir	child, kid
		小学	xiǎoxué	primary school

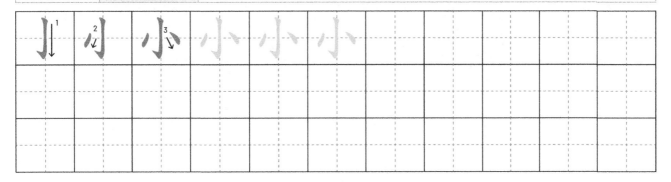

姐	jiě older sister	Common words:		
	8 strokes	小姐	xiǎojiě	Miss
	radical: 女	姐姐	jiějie	older sister
		姐妹	jiěmèi	sisters

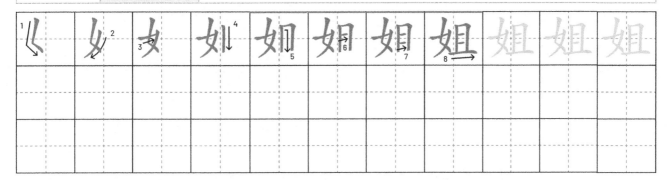

和	hé and, together	Common words:		
	8 strokes	我和你	wǒ hé nǐ	You and I
	radical: 禾	和平	hépíng	peace
		总和	zǒnghé	sum, total

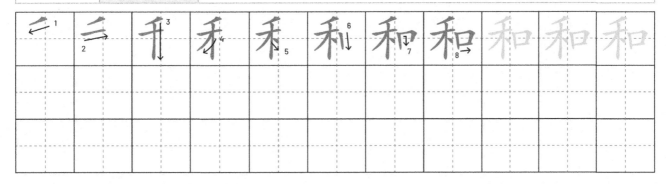

	zhōng	Common words:
	center, middle	中国　zhōngguó　China
	4 strokes	中间　zhōngjiān　middle
	radical: ｜	中文　zhōngwén　Chinese language

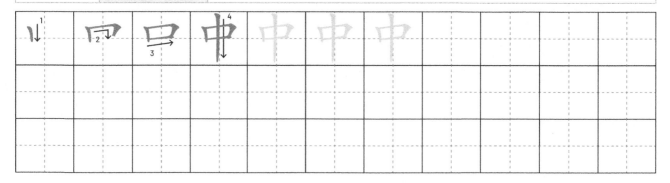

	guó	Common words:
	country, nation	国家　guójiā　country, state
	8 strokes	国外　guówài　abroad
	radical: 囗	国王　guówāng　king

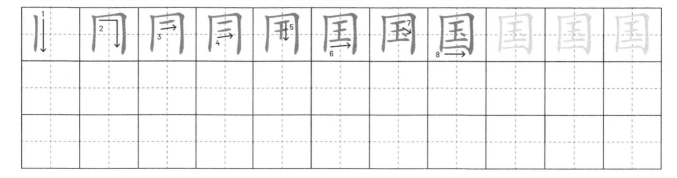

	rén	Common words:
	person, people	男人　nánrén　man
	2 strokes	女人　nǚrén　woman
	radical: 人	老人　lǎorén　elder people

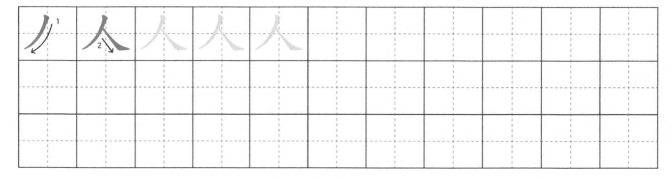

知	zhī	Common words:		
	to know	知道	zhīdào	to know, to recognize
	8 strokes	知识	zhīshi	knowledge
	radical: 矢	通知	tōngzhī	to notify, notice

道	dào	Common words:		
	road, path, way	道理	dàolǐ	reason, justification
	12 strokes	道路	dàolù	path
	radical: 辶	道教	Dàojiào	Daoism

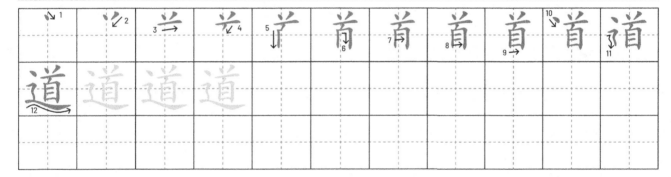

地	dì	Common words:		
	land, ground, place	地方	dìfang	place
	6 strokes	地球	dìqiú	Planet Earth
	radical: 土	地区	dìqū	region

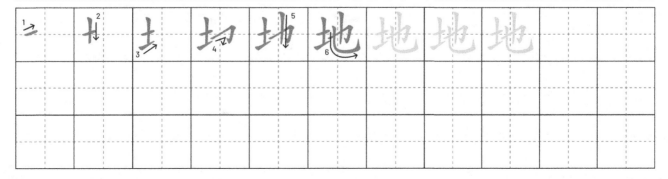

方	fāng	Common words:		
	direction, square	方向	fāngxiàng	direction
	4 strokes	方法	fāngfǎ	method, way
	radical: 方	四方	sìfāng	four directions, everywhere, square

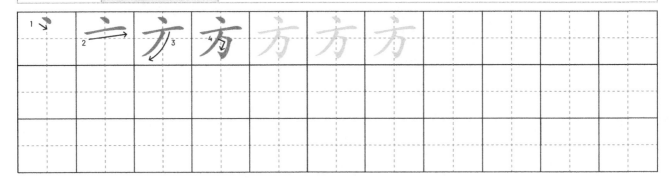

大	dà	Common words:		
	big, large, great	大小	dàxiǎo	size, measurement
	3 strokes	大号	dà hào	large size
	radical: 大	大学	dàxué	university

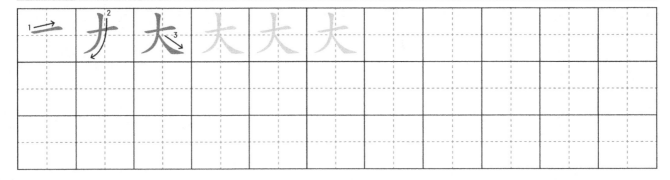

哪	nǎ/něi	Common words:		
	which	哪儿	nǎr	where
	9 strokes	哪里	nǎlǐ	where
	radical: 口	哪些	nǎxiē	which (ones)

WORD PRACTICE

这是 **zhè shì** this is

这	是								

那是 **nà shì** that is

那	是								

先生 **xiān sheng** Mr., husband

先	生								

太太 **tài tai** Mrs., wife

太	太								

小姐 **xiǎojiě** Miss

小	姐								

中国 **Zhōngguó** China

中	国								

知道 **zhīdào** to know, to be aware of

知	道								

地方 **dì fang** place

地	方								

1. Write down the corresponding Chinese characters in the brackets.

(   )   (   )   (   )   (   )   (   )

   shì   zhè/zhèi   nà/nèi   xiān   shēng

(   )   (   )   (   )   (   )   (   )

   tài   xiǎo   jiě   hé   Zhōng

(   )   (   )   (   )   (   )   (   )

   guó   rén   zhī   dào   dì

(   )   (   )   (   )

   fāng   dà   nǎ/něi

2. Choose the right character to make appropriate compound words.

xiāng	jiě	guó	zhī	fāng	hé	tài
先	姐	国	知	方	和	太

____生, ____太, 小____, 先生____太太, 中____人, ____道, 地____

3. Please write the corresponding Chinese Characters.

1) Zhè xiānsheng shì Zhōngguó rén.

_____

2) Nà xiǎojiě bú shì Zhōngguó rén.

_____

3) Nǐ shì Zhōngguó shěn me dìfāng rén?

_____.

4) Nǐ zhīdào Zhōngguó ma?

_____.

4. **Rearrange the word order to form correct sentences.**

1) 中人我是们国。

_____

2) 是小她太，不姐是太。

_____

3) 地方你么什中国是人？

_____

3) 中道知国她。

_____

5. **Listening practice: Please listen to the audio and choose the words/sentences you have heard in each group.**

1) A. 先生	B. 太太	C. 小姐
2) A. 我们是中国人。	B. 你们是中国人。	C. 我们不是中国人。
3) A. 什么地方人？	B. 什么国人？	C. 什么人？
4) A. 我知道中国。	B. 我们知道中国。	C. 她知道中国。

WHAT DATE IS IT TODAY? | 今天几号？

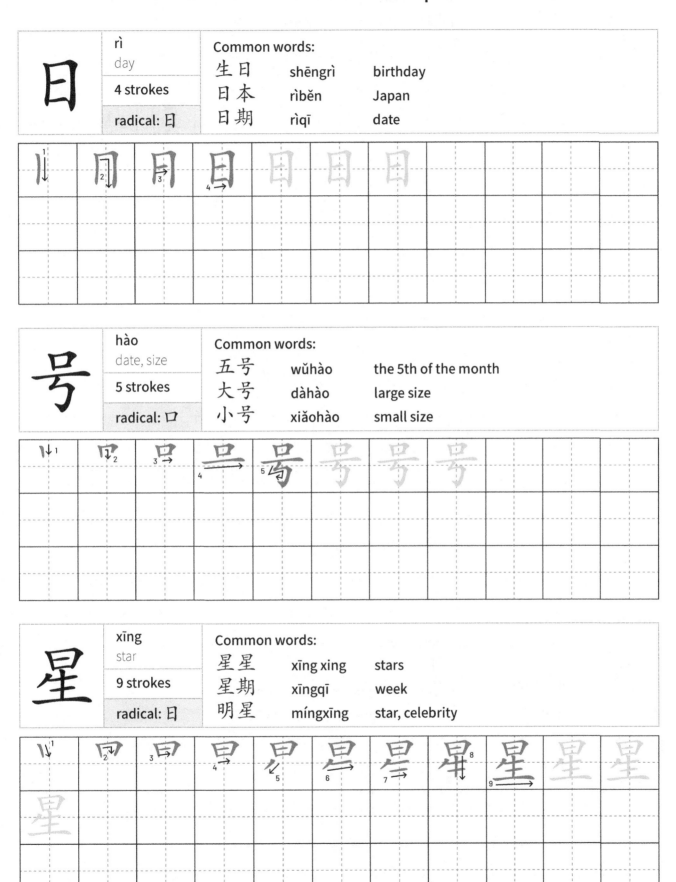

日	rì	Common words:		
	day	生日	shēngrì	birthday
	4 strokes	日本	rìběn	Japan
	radical: 日	日期	rìqī	date

号	hào	Common words:		
	date, size	五号	wǔhào	the 5th of the month
	5 strokes	大号	dàhào	large size
	radical: 口	小号	xiǎohào	small size

星	xīng	Common words:		
	star	星星	xīng xing	stars
	9 strokes	星期	xīngqī	week
	radical: 日	明星	míngxīng	star, celebrity

期	qī period of time	Common words:		
	12 strokes	日期	rìqī	date
		星期	xīngqī	week
	radical: 月	时期	shíqī	period

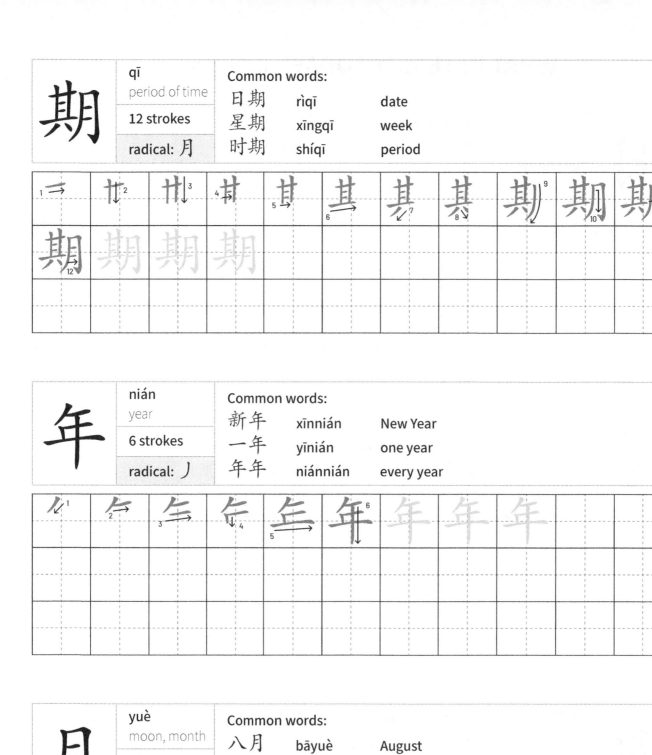

年	nián year	Common words:		
	6 strokes	新年	xīnnián	New Year
		一年	yīnián	one year
	radical: 丿	年年	niánnián	every year

月	yuè moon, month	Common words:		
	4 strokes	八月	bāyuè	August
		月球	yuèqiú	the Moon
	radical: 月	月光	yuèguāng	moonlight

天	tiān	Common words:		
	day, sky	明天	míngtiān	tomorrow
	4 strokes	天天	tiāntiān	every day
	radical: 一	天气	tiānqì	weather

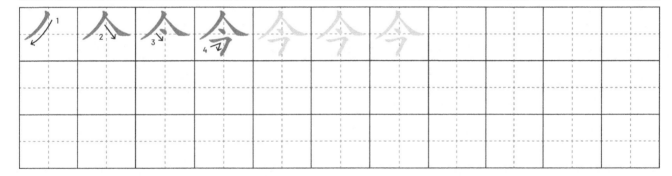

今	jīn	Common words:		
	present	今天	jīntiān	today
	4 strokes	今年	jīnnián	this year
	radical: 人	现今	xiànjīn	nowadays

明	míng	Common words:		
	bright	明天	míngtiān	tomorrow
	8 strokes	明月	míngyuè	bright moon
	radical: 日	明白	míngbai	clear

后	hòu behind, back	Common words:		
	6 strokes	后天	hòutiān	the day after tomorrow
	radical: 口	后来	hòulái	later, afterwards
		后边	hòubiān	behind, back

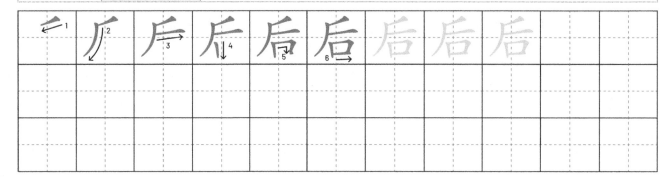

昨	zuó yesterday	Common words:		
	9 strokes	昨天	zuótiān	yesterday
	radical: 日	昨日	zuórì	yesterday
		昨儿	zuór	yesterday

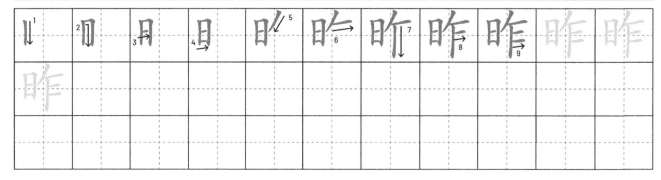

前	qián before, front	Common words:		
	9 strokes	前天	qiántiān	the day before yesterday
	radical: 丷	前年	qiánnián	the year before last year
		前边	qiánbiān	front

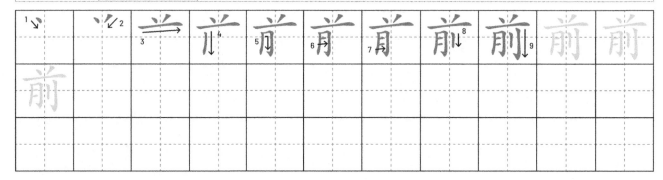

新	xīn
	new
	13 strokes
	radical: 斤

Common words:

新年	xīnnián	the New Year
新生	xīnshēng	new student
新加坡	Xīnjiāpō	Singapore

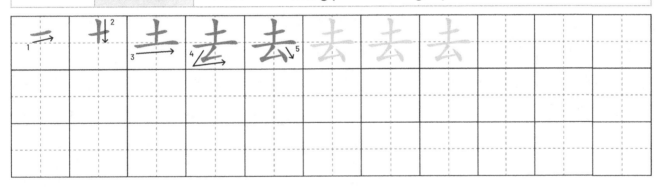

去	qù
	to go, past
	5 strokes
	radical: 土

Common words:

过去	guòqù	past
去商店	qù shāngdiàn	go to shops
上去	shàngqu	go up

多	duō
	many, much
	6 strokes
	radical: 夕

Common words:

很多	hěn duō	many, much
不多	bù duō	not many, not much
多少	duōshǎo	how many? how much?

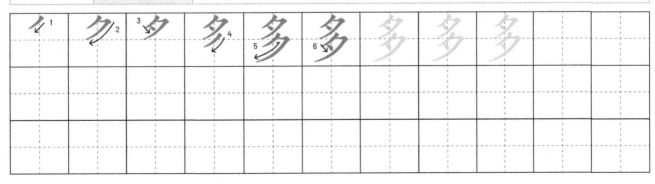

少	shǎo *few*	Common words:		
		很少	hěn shǎo	few, little
	4 strokes	不少	bù shǎo	not a few, a lot
	radical: 小	少见	shǎo jiàn	rare to see

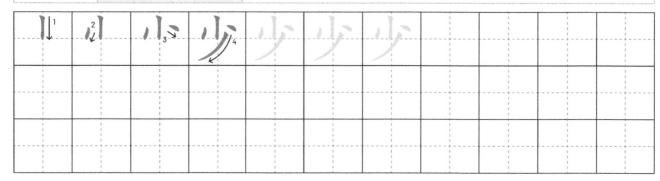

几	jǐ *how many, how much*	Common words:		
		几个	jǐgè	several, some
	2 strokes	没几个	méi jǐgè	few, almost none
	radical: 几	几乎	jīhū	almost, nearly

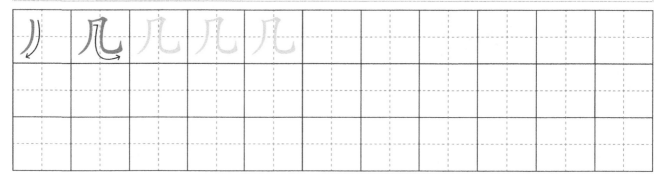

岁	suì *year (age)*	Common words:		
		三岁	sān suì	three years old
	6 strokes	岁数	suìshu	age
	radical: 山	岁月	suìyuè	time period, era

WORD PRACTICE

星期 **xīngqī** week

星	期								

今天 **jīntiān** today

今	天								

明天 **míngtiān** tomorrow

明	天								

后天 **hòutiān** the day after tomorrow

后	天								

昨天 **zuótiān** yesterday

昨	天								

前天 **qiántiān** the day before yesterday

前	天								

今年 **jīnnián** this year

今	年							

明年 **míngnián** next year

明	年							

后年 **hòunián** the year after next year

后	年							

去年 **qùnián** last year

去	年							

前年 **qiánnián** the year before last year

前	年							

新年 **xīnnián** New Year

新	年							

多少 **duōshǎo** how many, how much

多	少							

EXERCISE SET 5 练习5

WHAT DATE IS IT TODAY? 今天几号?

1. Write down the corresponding Chinese characters for the pinyin below.

(   )   (   )   (   )   (   )   (   )

   rì   hào   xīng   qī   nián

(   )   (   )   (   )   (   )   (   )

  yuè   tiān   jīn   míng   hòu

(   )   (   )   (   )   (   )   (   )

  zuó   qián   xīn   qù   duō

(   )   (   )   (   )

 shǎo   jǐ   suì

2. Look at the images below, please write down the corresponding sentences in Chinese.

TODAY IS MONDAY

_____

TOMORROW IS

AUGUST 7

_____

_____

HAPPY NEW YEAR _____

_____

3. Fill in the correct characters to complete the sentences.

1) 前天是八月十四号，星期六。

昨天是 (　　　　)月 (　　　　)号，星期 (　　　　)。

今天是(　　　　)月(　　　　) 号，星期(　　　　)。

2) 今年是二零二一年，

去年是 (　　　　)年。明年是(　　　　)年。

3) 后天是九月十号，星期二。

　　明天是(　　　)月(　　　)号，星期(　　　)。

　　前天是(　　　)月(　　　)号，星期(　　　)。

4. Rewrite the sentences in Chinese characters.

　　1) What date is it today? Today is the 16th of August.

　　_____.

　　2) What day is it today? Today is Monday.

　　_____.

　　3) The day after tomorrow is Wednesday.

　　_____.

　　4) Yesterday was the 4th of July.

　　_____.

 5. Listening practice: Please listen to the audio and choose the words/sentences you have heard in each group.

1) A. 今年是1990年。　　B. 明年是1990年。　　c. 后年是1990年。

2) A. 昨天是星期二。　　B. 昨天是星期三。　　c. 昨天是星期四。

3) A. 她去年二十五岁。　　B. 她去年三十五岁。　　c. 她去年四十五岁。

4) A. 今天是星期四，　　B. 今天是星期三，　　c. 今天是星期二，
　　 十五号。　　　　　　　 十四号。　　　　　　　 十三号。

WHAT TIME IS IT NOW? | 现在几点了？

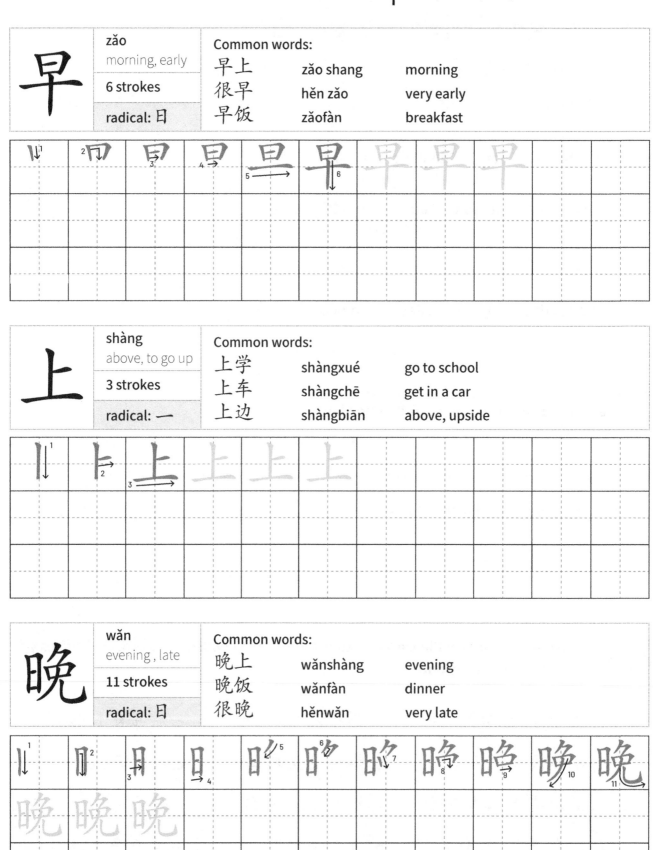

早	zǎo morning, early	Common words:		
	6 strokes	早上	zǎo shang	morning
		很早	hěn zǎo	very early
	radical: 日	早饭	zǎofàn	breakfast

上	shàng above, to go up	Common words:		
	3 strokes	上学	shàngxué	go to school
		上车	shàngchē	get in a car
	radical: 一	上边	shàngbiān	above, upside

晚	wǎn evening, late	Common words:		
	11 strokes	晚上	wǎnshàng	evening
		晚饭	wǎnfàn	dinner
	radical: 日	很晚	hěnwǎn	very late

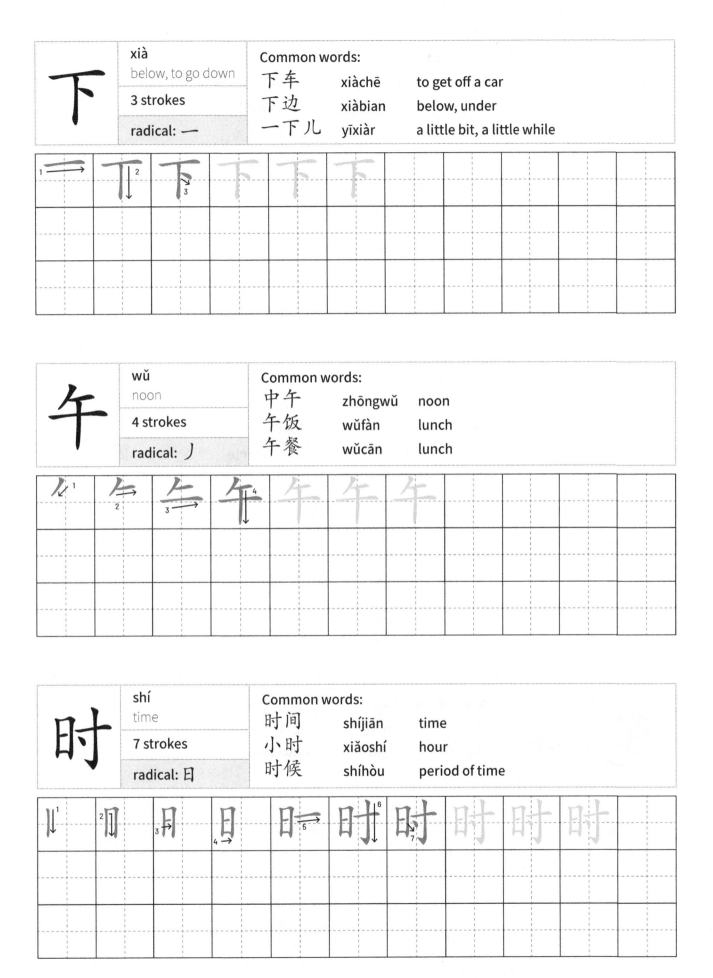

下	xià below, to go down	Common words:
	3 strokes	下车　　xiàchē　　to get off a car 下边　　xiàbian　　below, under 一下儿　yīxiàr　　a little bit, a little while
	radical: 一	

午	wǔ noon	Common words:
	4 strokes	中午　　zhōngwǔ　　noon 午饭　　wǔfàn　　lunch 午餐　　wǔcān　　lunch
	radical: 丿	

时	shí time	Common words:
	7 strokes	时间　　shíjiān　　time 小时　　xiǎoshí　　hour 时候　　shíhòu　　period of time
	radical: 日	

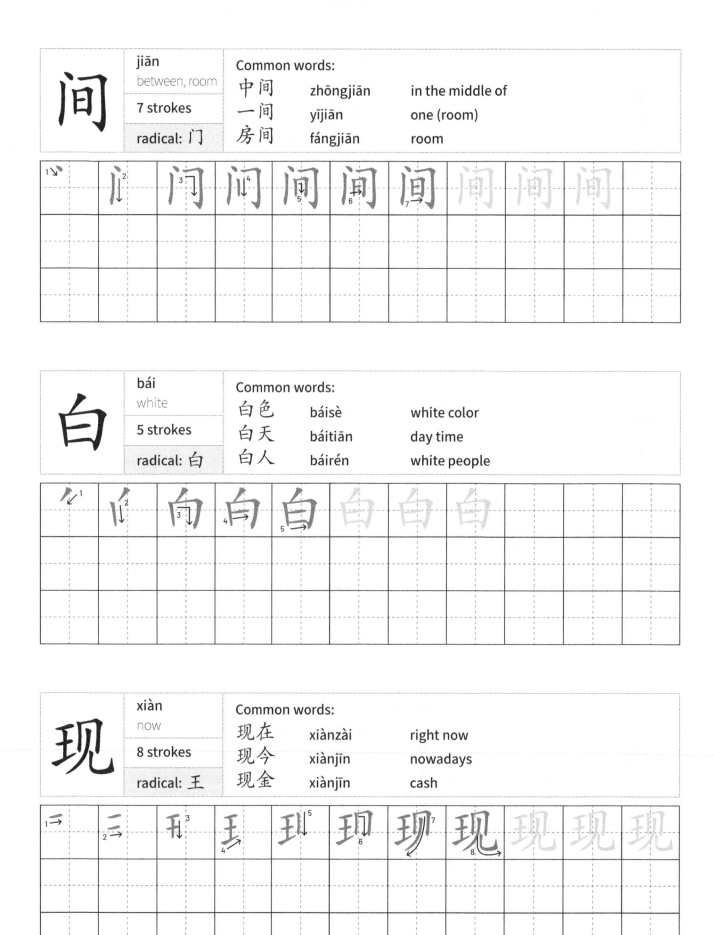

间	jiān
	between, room
	7 strokes
	radical: 门

Common words:

中间	zhōngjiān	in the middle of
一间	yījiān	one (room)
房间	fángjiān	room

白	bái
	white
	5 strokes
	radical: 白

Common words:

白色	báisè	white color
白天	báitiān	day time
白人	báirén	white people

现	xiàn
	now
	8 strokes
	radical: 王

Common words:

现在	xiànzài	right now
现今	xiànjīn	nowadays
现金	xiànjīn	cash

在	zài to be (in, at, on)	Common words:		
	6 strokes	现在	xiànzài	right now
		住在	zhù zài	live in/on/at
	radical: 土	在家	zàijiā	at home

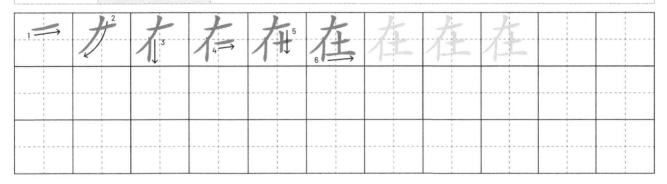

差	chà to lack	Common words:		
	9 strokes	很差	hěn chà	very bad
		差五分钟	chà wǔfēnzhōng	five minutes short
	radical: 工	差不多	chàbuduō	almost, nearly

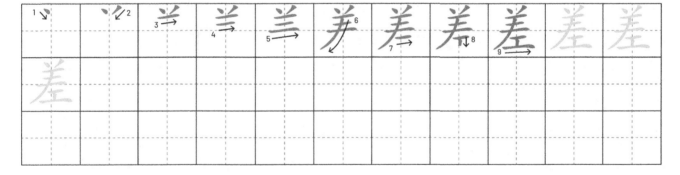

分	fēn minute	Common words:		
	4 strokes	五分钟	wǔfēnzhōng	five minutes
		分数	fēnshù	grade
	radical: 八	五分钱	wǔfēnqián	five cents

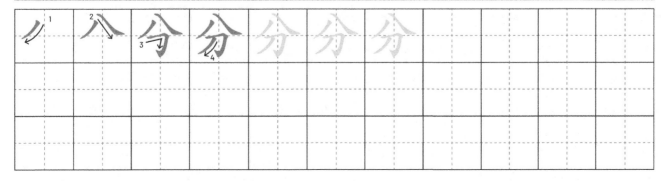

点	diǎn		Common words:		
	dot, o'clock		两点	liǎngdiǎn	two o' clock
	9 strokes		点菜	diǎncài	to order dish
	radical: 灬		一点儿	yīdiǎnr	a little bit

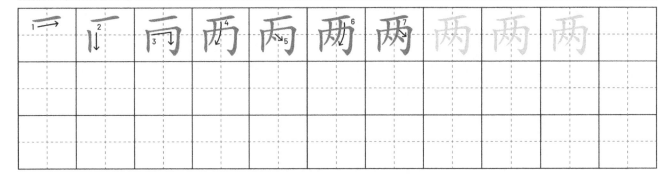

两	liǎng		Common words:		
	two		两点	liǎngdiǎn	two o'clock
	7 strokes		两个	liǎnggè	two of
	radical: 一		两人	liǎngrén	two people

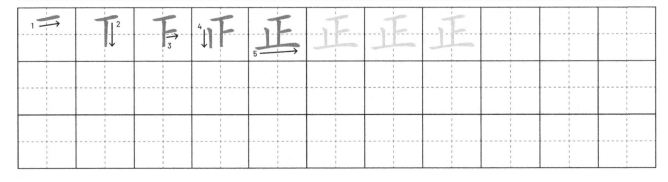

正	zhèng		Common words:		
	just		正在	zhèngzài	now
	5 strokes		正常	zhèngcháng	ordinary, normal
	radical: 一		正确	zhèngquè	correct

候	hòu time, to wait	Common words:		
	10 strokes	时候	shíhou	time period
	radical: 亻	问候	wènhòu	to greet
		候车	hòuchē	to wait for boarding

了	le/liǎo a particle	Common words:		
	2 strokes	几点了	jǐdiǎn le	what time is it?
	radical: 亅	看了	kàn le	have seen
		好了	hǎo le	all right

WORD PRACTICE

早上 **zǎo shang** morning

早	上							

晚上 **wǎn shang** evening

晚	上							

上午 **shàngwǔ** morning

上	午							

中午 **zhōngwǔ** noon

中	午							

下午 **xiàwǔ** afternoon

下	午							

白天 **báitiān** day time

白	天							

时间 **shíjiān** time

时	间								

中间 **zhōngjiān** in the middle

中	间								

正在 **zhèngzài** right now

正	在								

现在 **xiànzài** now

现	在								

时候 **shíhou** time period

时	侯								

两点 **liǎngdiǎn** two o' clock

两	点								

差五分 **chà wǔfēn** five minutes to...

差	五	分							

1. **Write down the corresponding Chinese characters for the pinyin below.**

(   )   (   )   (   )   (   )   (   )

zǎo   shàng   wǎn   xià   wǔ

(   )   (   )   (   )   (   )   (   )

shí   jiān   bái   xiàn   zài

(   )   (   )   (   )   (   )   (   )

chà   fēng   diǎn   liǎng   zhèng

(   )   (   )

hòu   le

2. **Please read the pinyin and write the correct Chinese characters to complete the sentence.**

1) 现在是_____ (xiàwǔ) 三点钟。

    A. 今天   B. 下午   C. 上午

2) 现在_____ (chà) 五分八点。

    A. 差   B. 点   C. 钟

3) 我早上_____ (jiǔ) 点上班。

    A. 六   B. 八   C. 九

3. Look at the images below, please write down the corresponding sentences in Chinese.

_____.

_____.

_____.

_____.

4. Translate the following sentences in Chinese characters.

1) It is 2pm in the afternoon now.

_____.

2) What time is it now?

_____.

3) Is it 5pm? No, it is 10 to 5pm.

_____.

4) It is 8:45 in the morning now.

_____.

5. Listening practice: Please listen to the audio and choose the words/sentences you have heard in each group.

1) A. 现在几点了？   B. 正在几点了？   C. 今天几点了？

2) A. 现在是上午八点。   B. 现在是下午八点。   C. 现在是晚上八点。

3) A. 现在差五分八点。   B. 现在差五分九点。   C. 现在差十分八点。

4) A. 现在是什么时间？   B. 现在是什么时候？   C. 正在是什么时候？

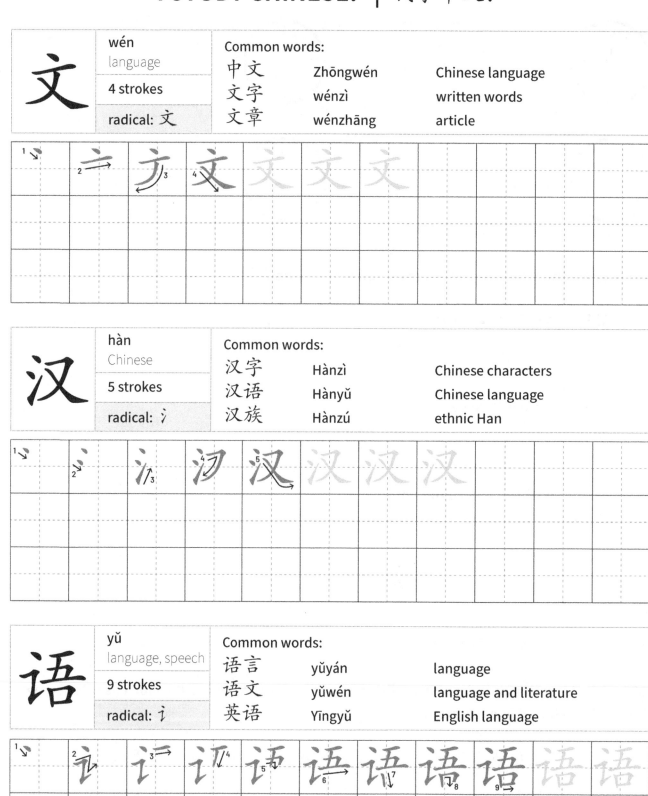

文	wén language	Common words:		
	4 strokes	中文	Zhōngwén	Chinese language
		文字	wénzì	written words
	radical: 文	文章	wénzhāng	article

汉	hàn Chinese	Common words:		
	5 strokes	汉字	Hànzì	Chinese characters
		汉语	Hànyǔ	Chinese language
	radical: 氵	汉族	Hànzú	ethnic Han

语	yǔ language, speech	Common words:		
	9 strokes	语言	yǔyán	language
		语文	yǔwén	language and literature
	radical: 讠	英语	Yīngyǔ	English language

外	wài	Common words:		
	foreign	外国	wàiguó	foreign countries
	5 strokes	外语	wàiyǔ	foreign languages
	radical: 夕	外衣	wàiyī	coat, jacket

学	xué	Common words:		
	to study	学习	xuéxí	to study
	8 strokes	学校	xuéxiào	school
	radical: 子	小学	xiǎoxué	primary school

习	xí	Common words:		
	to practice, to exercise	学习	xuéxí	to study
	3 strokes	习惯	xíguàn	habits
	radical: 〉	练习	liànxí	to practice

喜	xǐ
	to enjoy, happy, happiness
	12 strokes
	radical: 口

Common words:

喜欢　　xǐhuān　　to like, to be fond of
喜爱　　xǐ ài　　to love, favorite
喜好　　xǐhào　　to love, to be fond of, likes

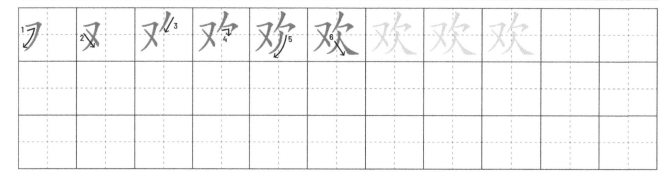

欢	huān
	happy, pleased
	6 strokes
	radical: 又

Common words:

喜欢　　xǐhuān　　to love, to be fond of
欢迎　　huānyíng　　to welcome, greeting
欢呼　　huānhū　　to hail, to cheer, cheer, jubilation

读	dú
	to read
	10 strokes
	radical: 讠

Common words:

读书　　dúshū　　to read books, to study
读一读　　dú yī dú　　to read a bit
朗读　　lǎngdú　　to read aloud

看	kàn	Common words:		
	to look, to read, to watch, to visit	看书	kàn shū	to read books
	9 strokes	看电视	kàn diànshì	to watch TV
	radical: 目	看妈妈	kàn māma	to visit mom

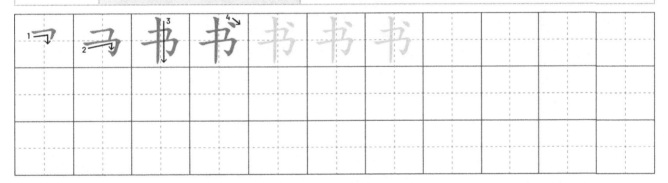

书	shū	Common words:		
	book	书本	shūběn	textbook
	4 strokes	书包	shūbāo	school bag
	radical: 乙	读书	dúshū	to read books, to read aloud

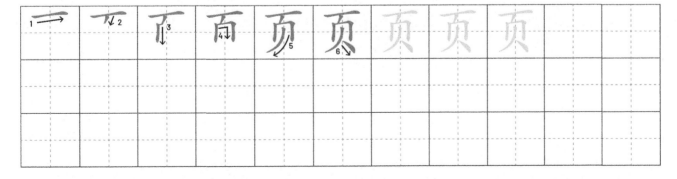

页	yè	Common words:		
	page	一页	yīyè	one page
	6 strokes	第三页	dì sān yè	the third page
	radical: 页	页码	yèmǎ	page number

说	shuō to speak	Common words:		
	9 strokes	说话	shuōhuà	to speak, to talk
		说说	shuō shuo	to talk about
	radical: 讠	说谎	shuōhuǎng	to tell a lie

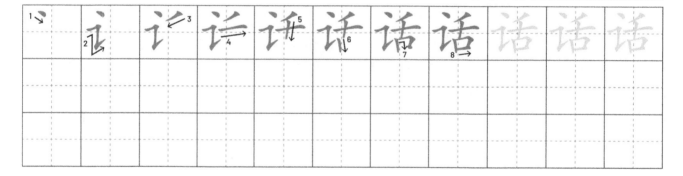

话	huà words, speech	Common words:		
	8 strokes	上海话	Shànghǎi huà	Shanghai dialect
		好话	hǎohuà	good words
	radical: 讠	会话	huìhuà	conversation

听	tīng to listen	Common words:		
	7 strokes	听歌	tīng gē	to listen to songs
		听话	tīnghuà	obedient
	radical: 口	听到	tīng dào	to hear

写	xiě	Common words:		
	to write	写字	xiě zì	to write characters
	5 strokes	写作	xiězuò	writing
	radical: 冖	编写	biānxiě	to write, to compile

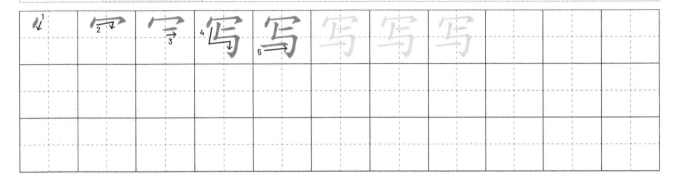

错	cuò	Common words:		
	wrong	对错	duì cuò	right and wrong
	13 strokes	错了	cuò le	to be wrong
	radical: 钅	错误	cuòwù	mistake, errors

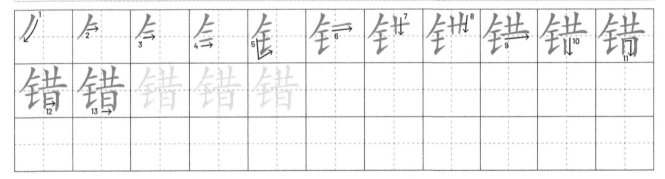

难	nán	Common words:		
	difficult, hard	很难	hěn nán	very difficult
	10 strokes	难易	nán yì	difficult and easy
	radical: 又	难处	nánchù	difficulty

真	zhēn true, truly, real, really	Common words:		
	10 strokes	真的	zhēn de	true, real
		真人	zhēn rén	real person
	radical: 十	真热	zhēn rè	so hot

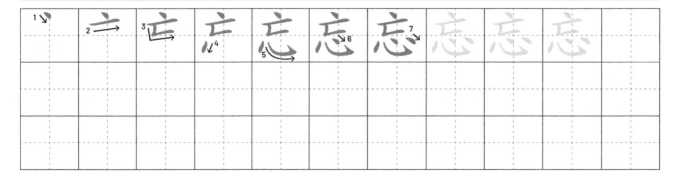

忘	wàng to forget	Common words:		
	7 strokes	忘记	wàngjì	to forget
		忘了	wàng le	forgot, forgotten
	radical: 心	忘我	wàngwǒ	to be selfless

记	jì to remember, to write down	Common words:		
	5 strokes	笔记	bǐjì	notes
		记得	jì de	to keep in memory, to remember
	radical: 讠	记忆	jìyì	memory

会	huì can, meeting	Common words:		
	6 strokes	会议	huìyì	meeting
		开会	kāihuì	to have meeting
	radical: 人	会开车	huì kāichē	to be able to drive

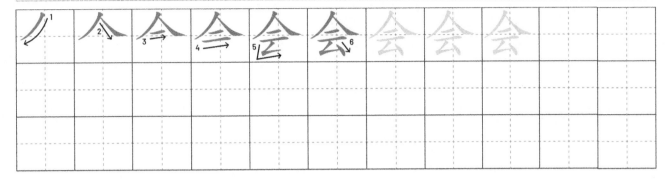

能	néng can, to be able to	Common words:		
	10 strokes	能人	néngrén	capable person
		可能	kěnéng	possible
	radical: 厶	能干	nénggàn	capable

用	yòng to use	Common words:		
	5 strokes	用人	yòng rén	servant, to make use of personnel
		使用	shǐyòng	to make use of, to employ
	radical: 用	费用	fèiyòng	expense, expenditure

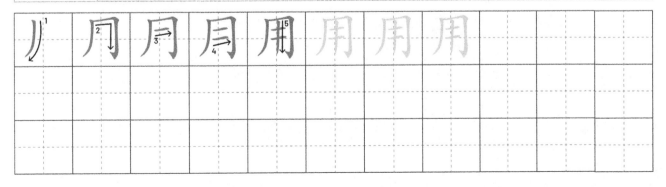

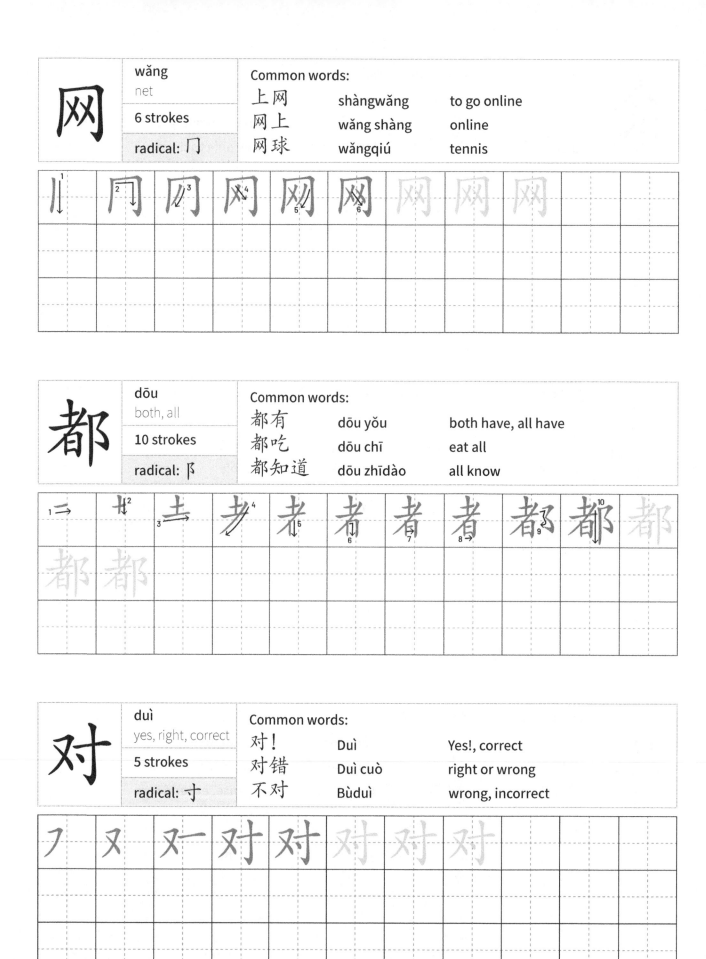

网	wǎng	Common words:		
	net	上网	shàngwǎng	to go online
	6 strokes	网上	wǎng shàng	online
	radical: 冂	网球	wǎngqiú	tennis

都	dōu	Common words:		
	both, all	都有	dōu yǒu	both have, all have
	10 strokes	都吃	dōu chī	eat all
	radical: 阝	都知道	dōu zhīdào	all know

对	duì	Common words:		
	yes, right, correct	对！	Duì	Yes!, correct
	5 strokes	对错	Duì cuò	right or wrong
	radical: 寸	不对	Bùduì	wrong, incorrect

WORD PRACTICE

中文 **Zhōngwén** Chinese language

中	文							

汉语 **Hànyǔ** Chinese language

汉	语							

外语 **wàiyǔ** foreign language

外	语							

写汉字 **xiě Hànzì** to write Chinese characters

写	汉	字						

学习 **xuéxí** to study

学	习							

读书 **dúshū** to study, to attend school

读	书							

看书 **kàn shū** to read books

看	书							

一页书 **yīyè shū** one page of a book

一	页	书						

说话 **shuōhuà** to speak, to talk

说	话							

写错 **xiě cuò** to write wrongly

写	错							

真的 **zhēn de** true, truly

真	的							

忘记 **wàngjì** to forget

忘	记							

上网 **shàngwǎng** to go online

上	网							

EXERCISE SET 7 练习7
I study Chinese! 我学中文!

1. **Write down the corresponding Chinese characters for the pinyin below.**

(   )   (   )   (   )   (   )   (   )

wén   hàn   yǔ   wài   zì

(   )   (   )   (   )   (   )   (   )

xué   xí   dú   kàn   shū

(   )   (   )   (   )   (   )   (   )

yè   shuō   huà   tīng   xiě

(   )   (   )   (   )   (   )   (   )

cuò   nán   zhēn   wàng   jì

(   )   (   )   (   )   (   )   (   )

huì   néng   yòng   wǎng   duì

2. **Please read the pinyin and write the correct Chinese characters to complete the sentence.**

1) 我现在_____ (xuéxí) 汉语。

    A. 学习   B. 学校   C. 学生

2) 他学写_____ (Hànzì)。

    A. 中文   B. 汉字   C. 汉语

3) 我早上看三＿＿＿＿ (yè) 书。

    A. 张   B. 本   C. 页

4) 她＿＿＿＿＿ (wàngjì) 小李的名字。

    A. 知道   B. 忘记   C. 记得

5) 我天天晚上都＿＿＿＿＿ (shàngwǎng)。

    A. 上网   B. 网上   C. 网球

3. **Construct sentences using the characters provided below.**

    Example: 写: 我早上写汉字。

    1) 学习: ＿＿＿＿＿＿＿＿＿＿＿＿＿＿＿＿＿＿＿＿

    2) 读: ＿＿＿＿＿＿＿＿＿＿＿＿＿＿＿＿＿＿＿＿

    3) 看: ＿＿＿＿＿＿＿＿＿＿＿＿＿＿＿＿＿＿＿＿

    4) 说: ＿＿＿＿＿＿＿＿＿＿＿＿＿＿＿＿＿＿＿＿

    5) 难: ＿＿＿＿＿＿＿＿＿＿＿＿＿＿＿＿＿＿＿＿

    6) 忘记: ＿＿＿＿＿＿＿＿＿＿＿＿＿＿＿＿＿＿＿＿

    7) 会: ＿＿＿＿＿＿＿＿＿＿＿＿＿＿＿＿＿＿＿＿

4. Translate the following sentences in Chinese characters.

1) He can speak foreign languages.

_____

2) I am able to speak the Chinese language.

_____

3) I write Chinese Characters every evening.

_____

4) He reads books.

_____

5) She listens to foreign languages in the morning.

_____

5. Listening practice: Please listen to the audio and choose the sentences you have heard in each group.

1) A. 我学习中文。   B. 我学习汉语。   C. 我学习外语。

2) A. 她晚上写汉字。   B. 她晚上写中文。   C. 她晚上写汉语。

3) A. 我和妈妈说话。   B. 我和妈妈看书。   C. 我和妈妈读书。

4) A. 我写错汉字。   B. 我写汉字。   C. 我读汉字。

5) A. 他忘记中文。   B. 他忘记上网。   C. 他忘记读书。

I LOVE SCHOOL! | 我爱学校！

爱	ài to love 10 strokes radical: ⻗	Common words: 喜爱　　　xǐ ài　　　　to like, to love 爱好　　　àihào　　　　hobby 恋爱　　　liàn' ài　　　to be in love

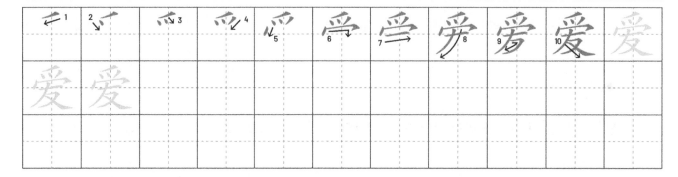

教	jiào / jiāo to teach 11 strokes radical: 攵	Common words: 教室　　　jiàoshì　　　classroom 教师　　　jiàoshī　　　teacher 教课　　　jiāo kè　　　to teach class

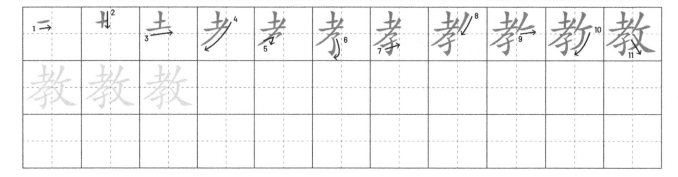

老	lǎo old, outdated 6 strokes radical: 耂	Common words: 老人　　　lǎorén　　　old people 老师　　　lǎoshī　　　teacher, master 老爸　　　lǎo bà　　　dad, father

师	shī teacher, master	Common words:		
	6 strokes	老师	lǎoshī	teacher, master
		师父	shīfu	master
	radical: 巾	师生	shīshēng	teachers and students

班	bān shift, class	Common words:		
	10 strokes	班级	bānjí	class
		早班	zǎobān	early shift
	radical: 王	晚班	wǎnbān	late shift

课	kè class, lesson	Common words:		
	10 strokes	课本	kèběn	textbooks
		上中文课	shàng Zhōngwén kè	to have a Chinese lesson
	radical: 讠	下课	xiàkè	to finish lesson, to finish class

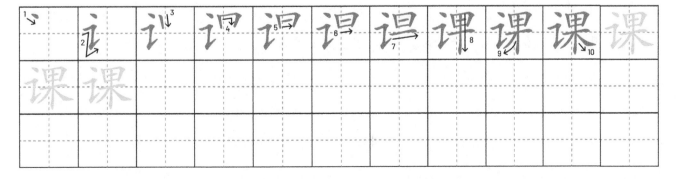

本	běn measure word for book, this, root, essence	Common words:		
	5 strokes	一本	yī běn	one (book, notebook)
		本周	běn zhōu	this week
	radical: 木	本质	běnzhì	essence, nature

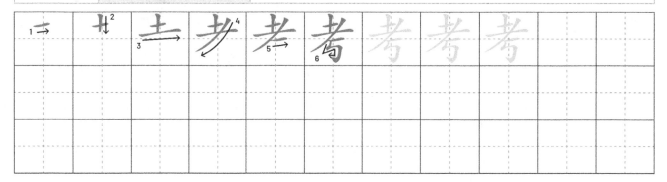

考	kǎo to test	Common words:		
	6 strokes	考试	kǎoshì	test, exam
		中考	zhōngkǎo	Senior High School Entrance Exam
	radical: 耂	高考	gāokǎo	College Entrance Exam

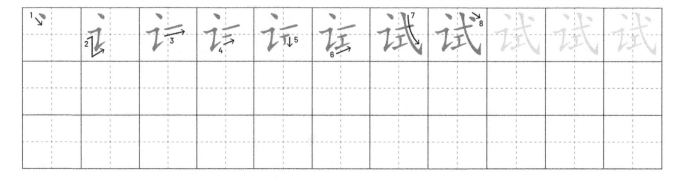

试	shì test, to try	Common words:		
	8 strokes	考试	kǎoshì	test, exam
		面试	miànshì	face to face interview
	radical: 讠	试试	shì shi	to try

准	zhǔn accurate, standard	Common words:		
	10 strokes	准备	zhǔnbèi	to prepare
		准确	zhǔnquè	accurate
	radical: 冫	标准	biāozhǔn	standard

备	bèi to prepare	Common words:		
	8 strokes	准备	zhǔnbèi	to prepare
		设备	shèbèi	equipment, device
	radical: 夂	装备	zhuāngbèi	equipment

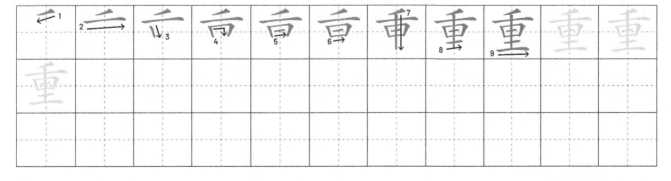

重	zhòng heavy	Common words:		
	9 strokes	重要	zhòngyào	important
		很重	hěn zhòng	very heavy
	radical: 丿	重点	zhòngdiǎn	emphasis, main point

要	yào to want	Common words:		
	9 strokes	重要	zhòngyào	important
		需要	xūyào	need, to need
	radical: 西	要求	yāoqiú	request, to request

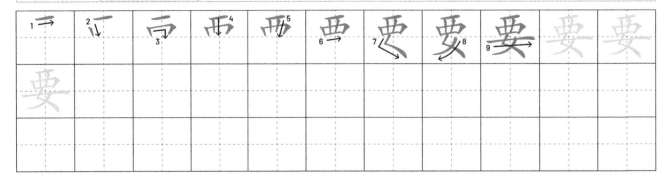

电	diàn electricity	Common words:		
	5 strokes	电话	diànhuà	telephone
		电视	diànshì	TV
	radical: 丨	电脑	diànnǎo	computer

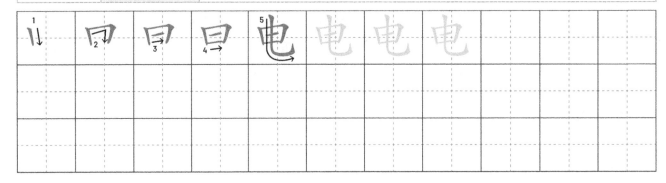

脑	nǎo brain	Common words:		
	10 strokes	电脑	diànnǎo	computer
		大脑	dànǎo	brain
	radical: 月	头脑	tóunǎo	brain, mind

影	yǐng shadow, film	Common words:		
	15 strokes	电影	diànyǐng	movie, film
		影子	yǐngzi	shadow
	radical: 彡	影响	yǐngxiǎng	influence

视	shì to see, to look at	Common words:		
	8 strokes	电视	diànshì	television
		视力	shìlì	vision, sight
	radical: 礻	视觉	shìjué	visual

跑	pǎo to run	Common words:		
	12 strokes	跑步	pǎobù	to run
		小跑	xiǎopǎo	to trot
	radical: 足	逃跑	táopǎo	to escape

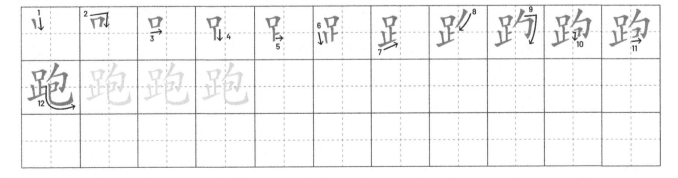

快	kuài _fast_	Common words:		
		快跑	kuài pǎo	to run fast
	7 strokes	快走	kuài zǒu	to walk fast
	radical: 忄	很快	hěn kuài	very fast

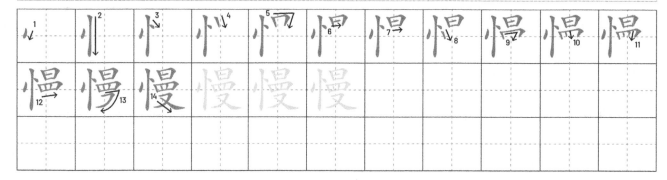

慢	màn _slow_	Common words:		
		慢跑	màn pǎo	to run slow
	14 strokes	慢走	màn zǒu	to walk slow
	radical: 忄	很慢	hěn màn	very slow

放	fàng _to place, to let out_	Common words:		
		放学	fàngxué	to let out of school
	8 strokes	放假	fàngjià	to let off of school or work
	radical: 攵	放心	fàngxīn	to set one's mind at rest

WORD PRACTICE

上班 **shàngbān** go to work

上	班							

上中文课 **shàng Zhōngwén kè** to have a Chinese lesson, to have Chinese class

上	中	文	课					

爱中文 **ài Zhōngwén** love Chinese language

爱	中	文						

教师 **jiàoshī** teacher

教	师							

课本 **kèběn** textbook

课	本							

准备 **zhǔnbèi** to prepare

准	备							

考试 **kǎoshì** exam, test

考	试							

重要 **zhòngyào** important

重	要							

电脑 **diànnǎo** computer

电	脑							

电影 **diànyǐng** film, movie

电	影							

快跑 **kuài pǎo** to run fast

快	跑							

慢跑 **màn pǎo** jogging, to jog

慢	跑							

放学 **fàngxué** to let out of school

放	学							

EXERCISE SET 8 练习8
I LOVE SCHOOL! 我爱学校!

1. **Write down the corresponding Chinese characters for the pinyin below.**

(　　　)　　　(　　　)　　　(　　　)　　　(　　　)　　　(　　　)

　ài　　　　　jiào　　　　　bān　　　　　kè　　　　　běn

(　　　)　　　(　　　)　　　(　　　)　　　(　　　)　　　(　　　)

　kǎo　　　　　shì　　　　　zhǔn　　　　　bèi　　　　　zhòng

(　　　)　　　(　　　)　　　(　　　)　　　(　　　)　　　(　　　)

　yào　　　　　diàn　　　　　nǎo　　　　　yǐng　　　　　pǎo

(　　　)　　　(　　　)　　　(　　　)

　kuài　　　　　màn　　　　　fàng

2. **Please read the pinyin and write the correct Chinese characters to complete the sentence.**

1) 我_____ (ài) 中文课。

   A. 学　　　　　　　B. 爱　　　　　　　C. 读

2) 他_____ (zhǔnbèi) 考试。

   A. 准备　　　　　　B. 学习　　　　　　C. 听写

3) 学中文很_____ (zhòngyào)。

   A. 好　　　　　　　B. 难　　　　　　　C. 重要

4) 我爱看_____ (diànnǎo) 和电影。

   A. 电脑　　　　　　B. 电视　　　　　　C. 电话

3. Construct sentences using the characters provided below.

Example: 准备: 我准备写汉字。

1) 爱: _____

2) 考试: _____

3) 重要: _____

4) 电脑: _____

5) 电影: _____

6) 跑: _____

4. Translate the following sentences in Chinese characters.

1) I love Chinese language classes.

_____.

2) He reads two foreign language books tonight.

_____.

3) We prepare a Chinese language test.

_____.

4) We watch a Chinese movie on Saturdays.

_____.

5) I use a computer to go online.

_____.

5. Listening practice: Please listen to the audio and choose the sentences you have heard in each group.

1) **A.** 我爱学习中文。   **B.** 我爱学习汉语。   **C.** 我爱学习外语。

2) **A.** 我明天上中文课。   **B.** 我今天上中文课。   **C.** 我昨天上中文课。

3) **A.** 我用电脑上网。   **B.** 我用电脑网上。   **C.** 我用电影上网。

4) **A.** 他们明天准备考试。 **B.** 他们明天看电影。   **C.** 他们明天上网。

THERE ARE SIX PEOPLE IN MY FAMILY. | 我家有六口人。

家	jiā family, house	Common words:		
	10 strokes	我家	wǒ jiā	my family
		家庭	jiātíng	family, household
	radical: 宀	作家	zuòjiā	writer

妹	mèi younger sister	Common words:		
	8 strokes	妹妹	mèi mei	younger sister
		小妹	xiǎo mèi	little sister
	radical: 女	小妹夫	xiǎo mèifu	the husband of the little sister

哥	gē older brother	Common words:		
	10 strokes	哥哥	gēge	older brother
		大哥	dàgē	the oldest brother
	radical: 口	哥们	gēmen	buddies

弟	dì younger brother	Common words:		
	7 strokes	弟弟	dìdi	younger brother
		小弟	xiǎodì	little brother
	radical: 丷	堂弟	tángdì	a younger male patrilineal cousin

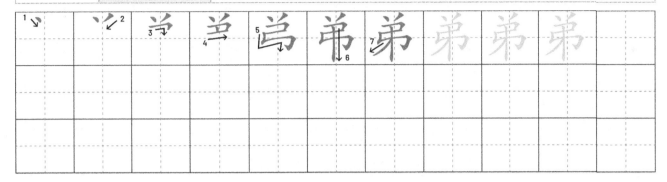

儿	er child, son	Common words:		
	2 strokes	儿子	ér zi	son
		小孩儿	xiǎoháir	kids, children
	radical: 儿	女儿	nǚ' ér	daughter

子	zi son, person, seed	Common words:		
	3 strokes	儿子	ér zi	son
		种子	zhǒng zi	seed
	radical: 子	小孩子	xiǎo háizi	kids, children

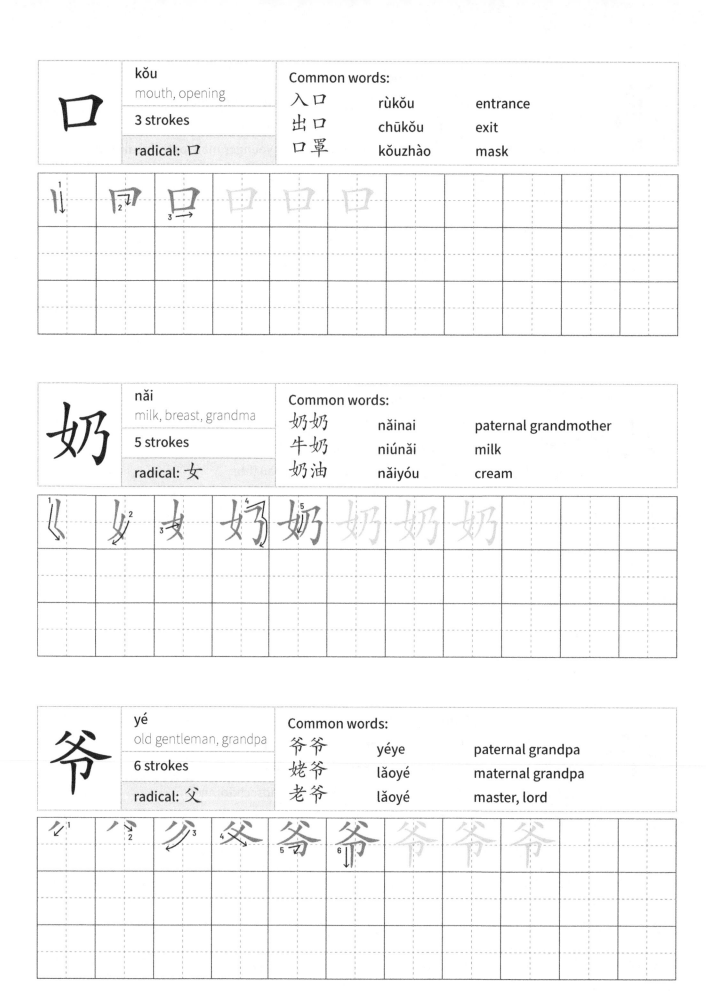

	kǒu mouth, opening 3 strokes radical: 口	Common words: 入口　　rùkǒu　　entrance 出口　　chūkǒu　　exit 口罩　　kǒuzhào　　mask

	nǎi milk, breast, grandma 5 strokes radical: 女	Common words: 奶奶　　nǎinai　　paternal grandmother 牛奶　　niúnǎi　　milk 奶油　　nǎiyóu　　cream

	yé old gentleman, grandpa 6 strokes radical: 父	Common words: 爷爷　　yéye　　paternal grandpa 姥爷　　lǎoyé　　maternal grandpa 老爷　　lǎoyé　　master, lord

妈	mā mom, mother	Common words:		
	6 strokes	妈妈	māma	mom, mother
		姨妈	yímā	aunt
	radical: 女	干妈	gānmā	godmother

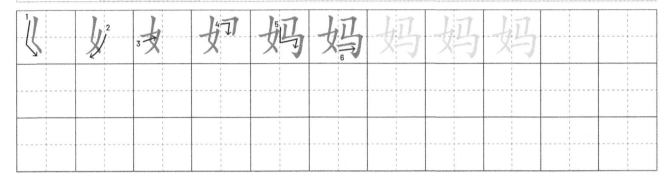

爸	bà dad, father	Common words:		
	8 strokes	爸爸	bàba	dad, father
		爸妈	bà mā	mom and dad, parents
	radical: 父	老爸	lǎo bà	dad, father

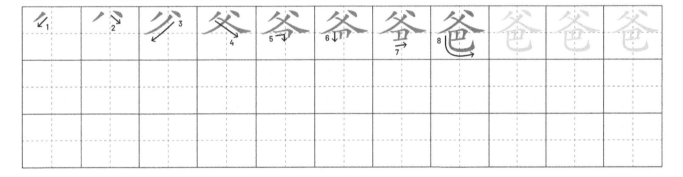

的	de a particle, of	Common words:		
	8 strokes	我的	wǒ de	my, mine
		真的	zhēn de	true, real
	radical: 白	他们的	tāmen de	their, theirs

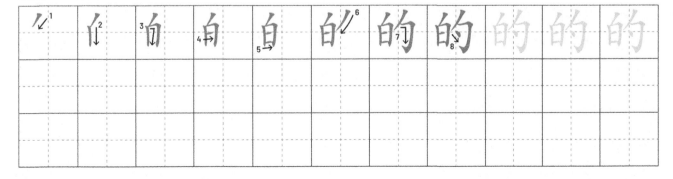

朋	péng companion	**Common words:**		
	8 strokes	朋友	péngyǒu	friend, pal
		男朋友	nán péngyǒu	boyfriend
	radical: 月	女朋友	nǚ péngyǒu	girlfriend

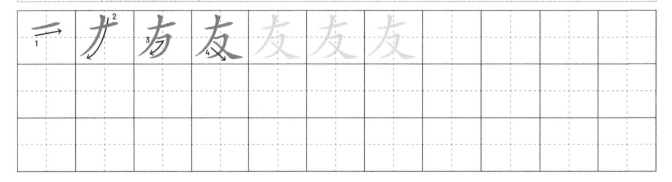

友	yǒu friendly	**Common words:**		
	4 strokes	朋友	péngyǒu	friend, pal
		友好	yǒuhǎo	friendly
	radical: 又	友善	yǒushàn	friendly and kind

有	yǒu to have, to has	**Common words:**		
	6 strokes	没有	méiyǒu	do not have
		有趣	yǒuqù	interesting, fun
	radical: 月	有些	yǒuxiē	some, several

没	méi not	Common words:		
	7 strokes	没有	méiyǒu	to not have
		没好处	méi hǎochù	no good, no benefit
	radical: 氵	没钱	méi qián	to not have money

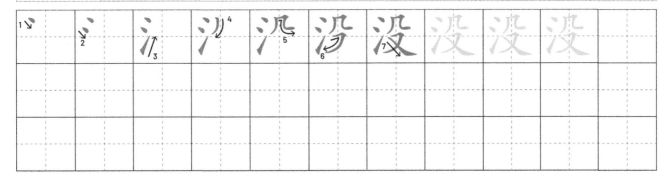

还	hái also, still, yet	Common words:		
	7 strokes	还没有	hái méiyǒu	still not have
		还好	háihǎo	alright, so so
	radical: 辶	还会	hái huì	also can

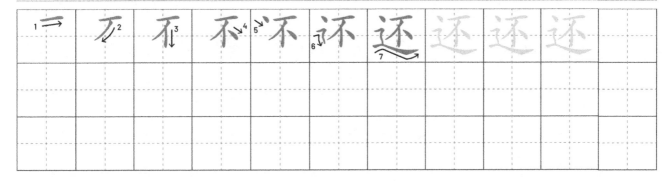

房	fáng house	Common words:		
	8 strokes	房子	fángzi	house
		房间	fángjiān	room
	radical: 户	双人房	shuāng rén fáng	double room

干	gān/gàn	Common words:		
	dry, to do	干净	gānjìng	clean
	3 strokes	干了	gān le	become dry
	radical: 一	干什么	gàn shénme	do what?

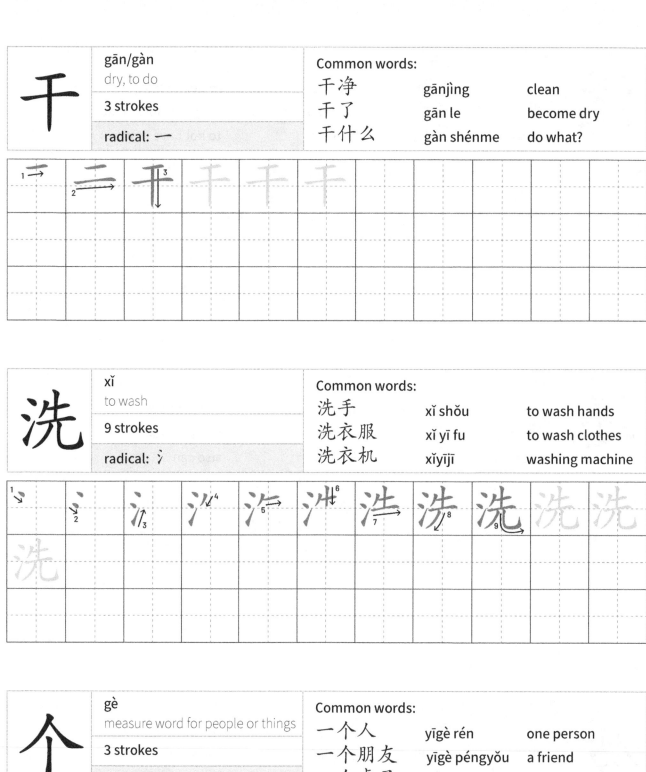

洗	xǐ	Common words:		
	to wash	洗手	xǐ shǒu	to wash hands
	9 strokes	洗衣服	xǐ yī fu	to wash clothes
	radical: 氵	洗衣机	xǐyījī	washing machine

个	gè	Common words:		
	measure word for people or things	一个人	yīgè rén	one person
	3 strokes	一个朋友	yīgè péngyǒu	a friend
	radical: 人	一个桌子	yīgè zhuō zi	a table

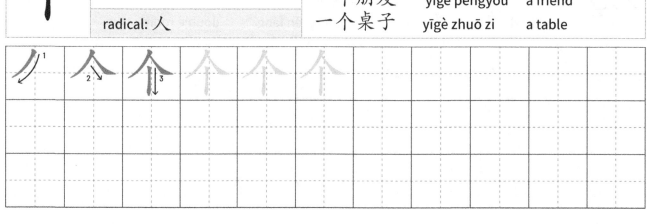

院	yuàn	Common words:		
	courtyard, institution	院子	yuàn zi	courtyard
	9 strokes	医院	yīyuàn	hospital
	radical: 阝	商学院	shāngxuéyuàn	business school

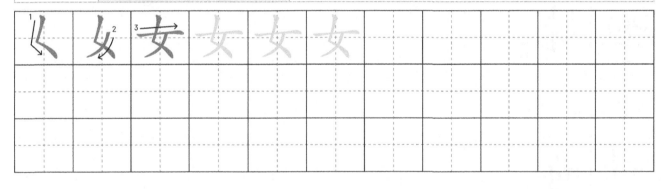

女	nǔ	Common words:		
	girl, daughter, female, woman	女儿	nǔ'ér	daughter
	3 strokes	女孩儿	nǔhái ér	girl
	radical: 女	女人	nǔrén	woman

WORD PRACTICE

家人 **jiārén** family member

家	人								

我的家人 **wǒ de jiārén** my family

我	的	家	人						

姐妹 **jiěmèi** sisters

姐	妹								

哥哥 **gēge** older brother

哥	哥								

弟弟 **dìdi** younger brother

弟	弟								

儿子 **ér zi** son

儿	子								

五口人 **wǔ kǒu rén** five family members

五	口	人							

一个朋友 **yīgè péngyǒu** a friend

一	个	朋	友						

男朋友 **nán péngyǒu** boyfriend

男	朋	友							

女朋友 **nǔ péngyǒu** girlfriend

女	朋	友							

没有 **méiyǒu** not to have, there is not, there are not

没	有								

还有 **háiyǒu** and also

还	有								

房子 **fáng zi** house

房	子								

干洗 **gānxǐ** dry cleaning

干	洗								

EXERCISE SET 9 练习9

THERE ARE SIX PEOPLE IN MY FAMILY. 我家有六口人。

1. Write down the corresponding Chinese characters for the pinyin below.

(   )   (   )   (   )   (   )   (   )

   jiā   jiě   mèi   gē   dì

(   )   (   )   (   )   (   )   (   )

   er   zi   kǒu   nǎi   yé

(   )   (   )   (   )   (   )   (   )

   péng   yǒu   yǒu   méi   hé

(   )   (   )   (   )   (   )   (   )

   hái   fáng   gàn   xǐ   de

(   )

   nǔ

2. Please read the pinyin and write the correct Chinese characters to complete the sentence.

1) 我家有五_____ (kǒu) 人。

    A. 口   B. 个   C. 本

2) 我有一个_____ (gē ge) 和两个姐姐。

    A. 弟弟   B. 哥哥   C. 妹妹

3) 他有三个儿子，_____ (méiyǒu) 女儿。

    A. 还有   B. 有   C. 没有

4) 他弟弟还没有_____ (nǚ péngyǒu) 呢！

    A. 男朋友   B. 女朋友   C. 朋友

5) 我家有三个_____ (fángzi)。

    A. 房子   B. 家子   C. 儿子

3. Translate the following sentences in Chinese characters.

1) There are five people in my family: mom, dad, an older brother, a younger brother and me.

_____.

2) She has a boyfriend. Her younger brother has a girlfriend.

_____.

3) My grandfather has three sons and two daughters.

_____.

4) His younger sister doesn' t have a boyfriend.

_____.

5) My family has three houses.

_____.

4. Listening practice: Please listen to the audio and choose the sentences you have heard in each group.

1) A. 我没有哥哥和弟弟。   B. 我没有姐姐和妹妹。   C. 我有哥哥和弟弟。

2) A. 我家有三口人。   B. 我家有三个人。   C. 我家有四口人。

3) A. 他没有朋友。   B. 他没有男朋友。   C. 他没有女朋友。

4) A. 他儿子没有姐姐。   B. 他儿子有姐姐。   C. 他儿子没有妹妹。

5) A. 我女儿没有爷爷。   B. 我女儿没有奶奶。   C. 我女儿没有姐姐。

CHINESE FOOD IS SO YUMMY! | 中国菜太好吃了!

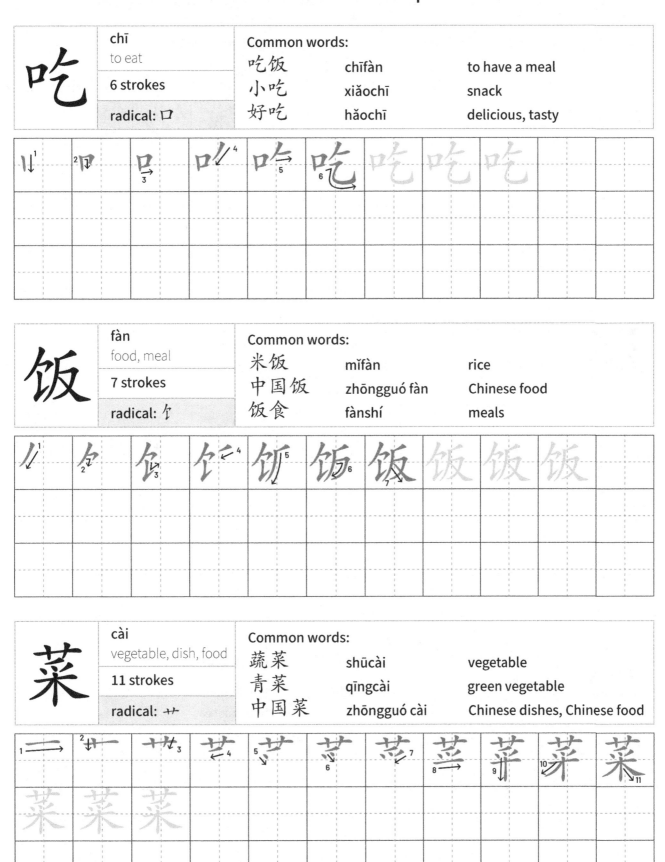

吃	chī		Common words:		
	to eat		吃饭	chīfàn	to have a meal
	6 strokes		小吃	xiǎochī	snack
	radical: 口		好吃	hǎochī	delicious, tasty

饭	fàn		Common words:		
	food, meal		米饭	mǐfàn	rice
	7 strokes		中国饭	zhōngguó fàn	Chinese food
	radical: 饣		饭食	fànshí	meals

菜	cài		Common words:		
	vegetable, dish, food		蔬菜	shūcài	vegetable
	11 strokes		青菜	qīngcài	green vegetable
	radical: 艹		中国菜	zhōngguó cài	Chinese dishes, Chinese food

饿	è hungry	Common words:		
	10 strokes	饿了	è le	starving
	radical: 饣	饥饿	jī'è	hunger, starvation
		肚子饿	dùzi è	hungry

渴	kě thirsty	Common words:		
	12 strokes	渴了	kě le	become thirsty
	radical: 氵	口渴	kǒukě	thirst
		不渴	bù kě	not thirsty

喝	hē to drink	Common words:		
	12 strokes	喝水	hēshuǐ	to drink water
	radical: 口	喝酒	hējiǔ	to drink alcohol
		喝茶	hēchá	to drink tea

水	shuǐ	Common words:		
	water	水果	shuǐguǒ	fruit
	4 strokes	喝水	hēshuǐ	to drink water
	radical: 水	山水	shānshuǐ	landscape

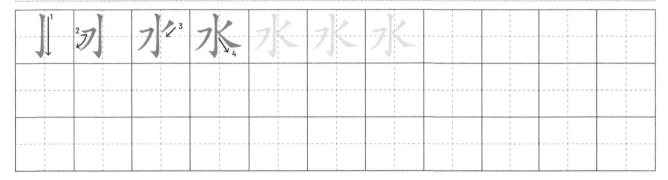

果	guǒ	Common words:		
	fruit	水果	shuǐguǒ	fruit
	8 strokes	苹果	píngguǒ	apple
	radical: 木	果实	guǒshí	fruit, fructification

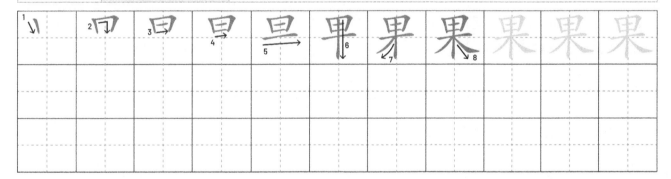

	xiǎng	Common words:		
	to think, would like	想一想	xiǎng yī xiǎng	to think about it
	13 strokes	想念	xiǎngniàn	to miss, to long for
	radical: 心	心想	xīnxiǎng	to think to oneself

茶	chá		Common words:		
	tea		泡茶	pàochá	to make tea
	9 strokes		绿茶	lǜchá	green tea
	radical: 艹		红茶	hóngchá	red tea

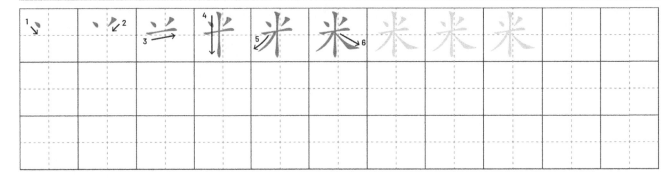

米	mǐ		Common words:		
	rice		大米	dàmǐ	rice
	6 strokes		米饭	mǐfàn	rice meal
	radical: 米		米粉	mǐfěn	rice noodle, rice flour

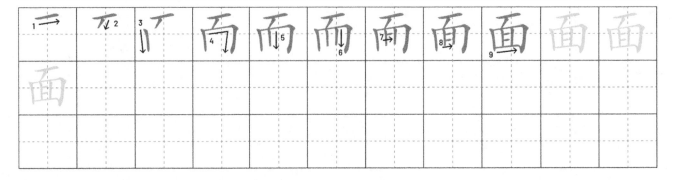

面	miàn		Common words:		
	flour		面条	miàntiáo	noodle
	9 strokes		面粉	miànfěn	flour
	radical: 一		面子	miàn zi	face, reputation

条	**tiáo** *measure word for thin & long things*	Common words:		
	7 strokes	一条狗	yī tiáo gǒu	a dog
	radical: 夊	一条河	yī tiáo hé	a river
		一条裤子	yī tiáo kù zi	a pair of trousers

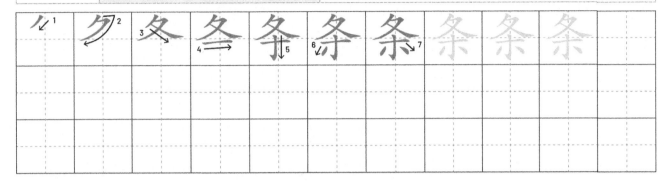

肉	**ròu** *meat*	Common words:		
	6 strokes	鸡肉	jīròu	chicken (meat)
	radical: 冂	牛肉	niúròu	beef
		羊肉	yángròu	lamb

包	**bāo** *steam stuffed bun, bag*	Common words:		
	5 strokes	包子	bāo zi	steamed stuffed bun
	radical: 勹	书包	shūbāo	school bag
		钱包	qiánbāo	wallet, purse

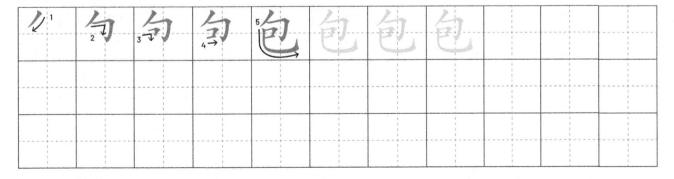

做	zuò to do	Common words:		
	11 strokes	做工	zuògōng	to do work
		做人	zuòrén	to conduct oneself
	radical: 亻	做作业	zuò zuòyè	to do homework

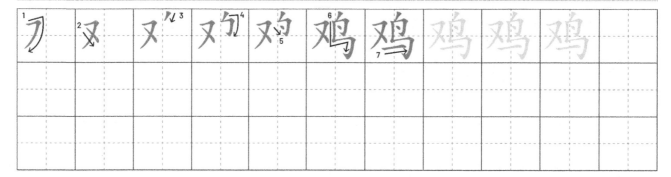

鸡	jī chicken, fowl	Common words:		
	7 strokes	鸡肉	jīròu	chicken (meat)
		小鸡	xiǎojī	spring chick
	radical: 又	老母鸡	lǎo mǔjī	old hen

蛋	dàn egg	Common words:		
	11 strokes	鸡蛋	jīdàn	egg
		坏蛋	huàidàn	evil person
	radical: 虫	蛋黄	dànhuáng	yolk

坏	huài	Common words:		
	out of order, bad	坏人	huàirén	bad person, evil person
	7 strokes	坏蛋	huàidàn	bad person, evil person
	radical: 土	坏了	huài le	broken, rotten

块	kuài	Common words:		
	piece	木块	mùkuài	wooden piece, block
	7 strokes	大块	dà kuài	a big piece, block
	radical: 土	小块	xiǎo kuài	a small piece, block

桌	zhuō	Common words:		
	table	书桌	shūzhuō	desk
	10 strokes	餐桌	cānzhuō	dining table
	radical: 木	桌面	zhuōmiàn	table surface

杯	bēi cup, glass	Common words:		
	8 strokes	杯子	bēi zi	cup, glass, mug
	radical: 木	一杯水	yī bēi shuǐ	a glass of water
		一杯茶	yī bēi chá	a cup of tea

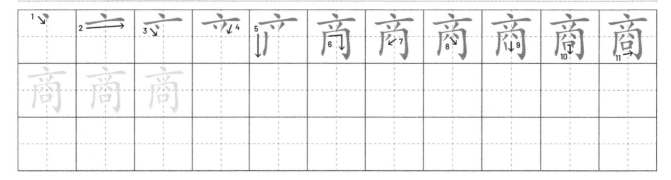

商	shāng business	Common words:		
	11 strokes	商人	shāngrén	businessman
	radical: 亠	商店	shāngdiàn	shop, store
		商学院	shāngxuéyuàn	business school

店	diàn shop	Common words:		
	8 strokes	商店	shāngdiàn	shop, store
	radical: 广	客店	kèdiàn	inn
		店名	diànmíng	name of a store

	guǎn place of cultural activities, building	Common words:		
	11 strokes	饭馆	fànguǎn	restaurant
		图书馆	túshūguǎn	library
	radical: 饣	博物馆	bówùguǎn	museum

WORD PRACTICE

中国饭/菜 **Zhōngguó fàn/cài** Chinese food, Chinese meal

中	国	饭	菜					

吃饭/菜 **chīfàn/cài** eat meal/dish

吃	饭	菜						

喝茶 **hēchá** drink tea

喝	茶							

水果 **shuǐguǒ** fruit

水	果							

米饭 **mǐfàn** rice

米	饭							

面条 **miàntiáo** noodles

面	条							

面包 **miànbāo** bread

面	包							

肉包子 **ròu bāo zi** steamed meat buns

肉	包	子						

做饭 **zuòfàn** to cook a meal

做	饭							

鸡蛋 **jīdàn** egg

鸡	蛋							

桌子 **zhuō zi** table

桌	子							

一块肉 **yī kuài ròu** a piece of meat

一	块	肉						

一杯茶 **yī bēi chá** a cup of tea

一	杯	茶						

商店 **shāngdiàn** shop, store

商	店								

图书馆 **túshūguǎn** library

图	书	馆							

1. **Write down the corresponding Chinese characters for the pinyin below.**

(   )   (   )   (   )   (   )   (   )

  chī   fàn   cài   è   kě

(   )   (   )   (   )   (   )   (   )

  hē   shuǐ   guǒ   xiǎng   chá

(   )   (   )   (   )   (   )   (   )

  mǐ   miàn   tiáo   ròu   bāo

(   )   (   )   (   )   (   )   (   )

  zuò   jī   dàn   huài   kuài

(   )   (   )   (   )

  zhuō   bēi   diàn

2. **Please read the pinyin and write the correct Chinese characters to complete the sentence.**

1) 我爱＿＿＿＿＿＿(chī)中国饭。

  A. 吃   B. 喝   C. 饿

2) 我想吃＿＿＿＿＿＿＿ (shuǐguǒ) 和鸡肉。

  A. 面条   B. 水果   C. 鸡蛋

3) 我今天做鸡蛋＿＿＿＿＿＿＿ (bāo zi)。

  A. 面条   B. 饭菜   C. 包子

4) 他想吃一_____ (kuài) 鸡肉。

    A. 块   B. 个   C. 杯

5) 我很渴，想_____ (hē) 一杯水。

    A. 吃   B. 喝   C. 做

3. Translate the following sentences in Chinese characters.

1) I will eat fruit and drink tea today.

_____

2) She would like to eat noodles tomorrow.

_____

3) I will cook egg rice tonight.

_____

4) He doesn' t want to eat rice, he would like to eat chicken.

_____

5) I would like to drink two glasses of Chinese tea.

_____

4. Listening practice: Please listen to the audio and choose the sentences you have heard in each group.

1) A. 我今天不吃面条。   B. 我今天吃面条。   C. 我今天不吃水果。

2) A. 他不想喝中国茶。   B. 他不想吃水果。   C. 他想喝中国茶。

3) A. 他想吃一块鸡肉。   B. 他想吃一块鸡蛋。   C. 他想吃一块水果。

4) A. 她晚上做鸡肉米饭。   B. 她晚上做鸡蛋米饭。   C. 她晚上做面条米饭。

5) A. 我想吃鸡肉包子。   B. 我想吃鸡肉面条。   C. 我想吃包子。

THE WEATHER TODAY IS VERY COLD. | 今天天气很冷。

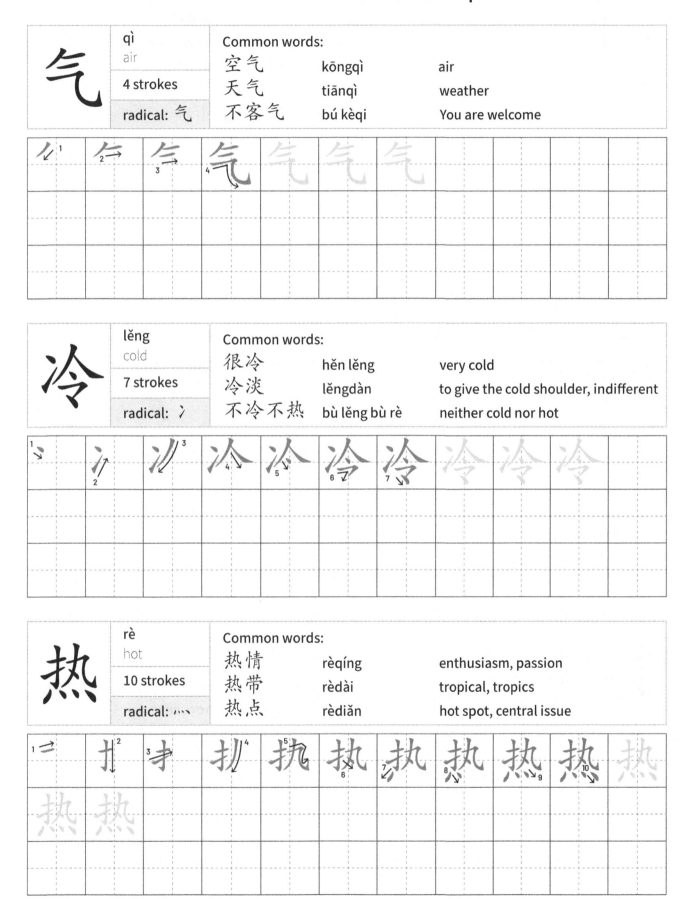

气	qì	Common words:		
	air	空气	kōngqì	air
	4 strokes	天气	tiānqì	weather
	radical: 气	不客气	bú kèqi	You are welcome

冷	lěng	Common words:		
	cold	很冷	hěn lěng	very cold
	7 strokes	冷淡	lěngdàn	to give the cold shoulder, indifferent
	radical: 冫	不冷不热	bù lěng bù rè	neither cold nor hot

热	rè	Common words:		
	hot	热情	rèqíng	enthusiasm, passion
	10 strokes	热带	rèdài	tropical, tropics
	radical: 灬	热点	rèdiǎn	hot spot, central issue

	yǔ rain	Common words:		
雨	8 strokes	下雨	xiàyǔ	to rain
		大雨	dàyǔ	heavy rain
	radical: 雨	毛毛雨	máo maoyǔ	drizzle

	zěn how, why	Common words:		
怎	9 strokes	怎么了	zěn me le	What happened?
		怎么样	zěn me yàng	How is it?
	radical: 心	怎么办	zěn me bàn	What to do?

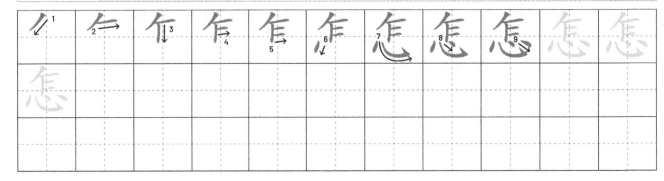

	yàng appearance, shape	Common words:		
样	10 strokes	这样	zhèyàng	so, like this, this way, such
		那样	nàyàng	so, like that, that way, such
	radical: 木	怎么样	zěn me yàng	how, why

	fēng wind	Common words:		
	4 strokes	大风	dàfēng	strong wind
	radical: 风	刮风	guāfēng	to be windy
		风景	fēngjǐng	scenery, landscape

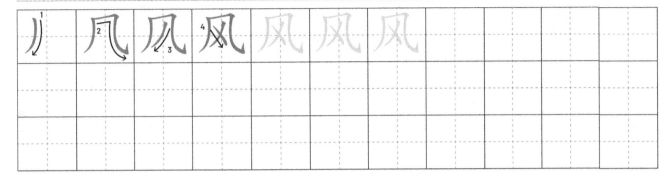

	zuì most, the most	Common words:		
	12 strokes	最好	zuìhǎo	the best
	radical: 日	最高	zuì gāo	the tallest
		最好吃	zuì hǎo chī	the most delicious

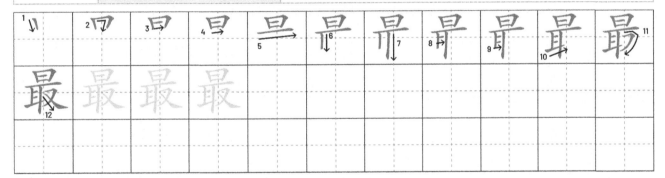

	bǐ particle used for comparison	Common words:		
	4 strokes	对比	duìbǐ	to compare, contrast
	radical: 比	比较	bǐjiào	to compare
		比如	bǐrú	for example

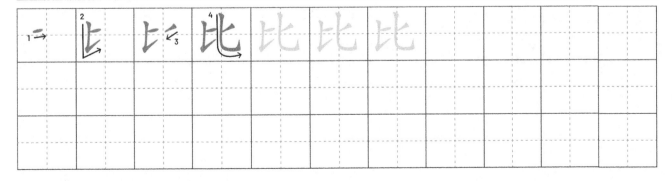

别	bié other, another, do not	Common words:		
	7 strokes	别人	biérén	other people
		别的	bié de	other
	radical: 刂	别吃	bié chī	Don' t eat!

别 别 别 别 别 别 别 别 别 别

跟	gēn to follow, to go with	Common words:		
	13 strokes	跟我	Gēn wǒ	with me
		跟从	Gēncóng	to follow
	radical: 足	跟班	Gēnbān	attendant

跟 跟 跟 跟 跟 跟 跟 跟 跟 跟 跟 跟 跟 跟 跟 跟

从	cóng from, to follow	Common words:		
	4 strokes	自从	zìcóng	since
		从事	cóngshì	to do, to handle
	radical: 人	跟从	gēncóng	to follow

从 从 从 从 从 从 从

WORD PRACTICE

天气 **tiānqì** weather

天	气								

不客气 **bù kèqi** You are welcome!

不	客	气							

不冷不热 **bù lěng bù rè** neither cold nor hot

不	冷	不	热						

下雨 **xiàyǔ** to rain

下	雨								

大风 **dàfēng** strong wind

大	风								

最热 **zuì rè** the hottest

最	热								

最冷 **zuì lěng** the coldest

最	冷							

别的 **bié de** other

别	的							

别人 **biérén** other people

别	人							

最冷 **zuì lěng** the coldest

EXERCISE SET 11 练习11

THE WEATHER TODAY IS VERY COLD. 今天天气很冷。

1. Write down the corresponding Chinese characters for the pinyin below.

(   )   (   )   (   )   (   )   (   )

    qì   lěng   rè   yǔ   zěn

(   )   (   )   (   )   (   )   (   )

   me   yàng   fēng   bǐ   zuì

(   )   (   )

   gēn   cóng

2. Please read the pinyin and write the correct Chinese characters to complete the sentence.

1) 今天_____ (tiānqì) 很热。

   A. 天气   B. 下雨   C. 有风

2) 昨天_____ (xiàyǔ) 了。

   A. 天气   B. 下雨   C. 有风

3) 明天天气_____ (zěn me yàng)?

   A. 怎么样   B. 有风   C. 下雨

4) 今天晚上_____ (yǒu fēng) 。

   A. 很热   B. 有风   C. 很冷

3. Look at the images below, then please write down the corresponding phrases/sentences in Chinese.

_____.

_____

_____.

4. Translate the following sentences in Chinese characters.

1) The weather today is very nice.

_____.

2) Tomorrow it will rain.

_____.

3) Yesterday there was no strong wind.

_____.

5. Listening practice: Please listen to the audio and choose the sentences you have heard in each group.

1) **A.** 今天不会下雨。   **B.** 今天没有风。   **C.** 今天有风。

2) **A.** 昨天天气很好。   **B.** 昨天天气很冷。   **C.** 昨天天气很热。

3) **A.** 明天天气怎么样？   **B.** 今天天气怎么样？   **C.** 昨天天气怎么样？

WHERE IS THE TRAIN STATION? | 火车站在哪儿?

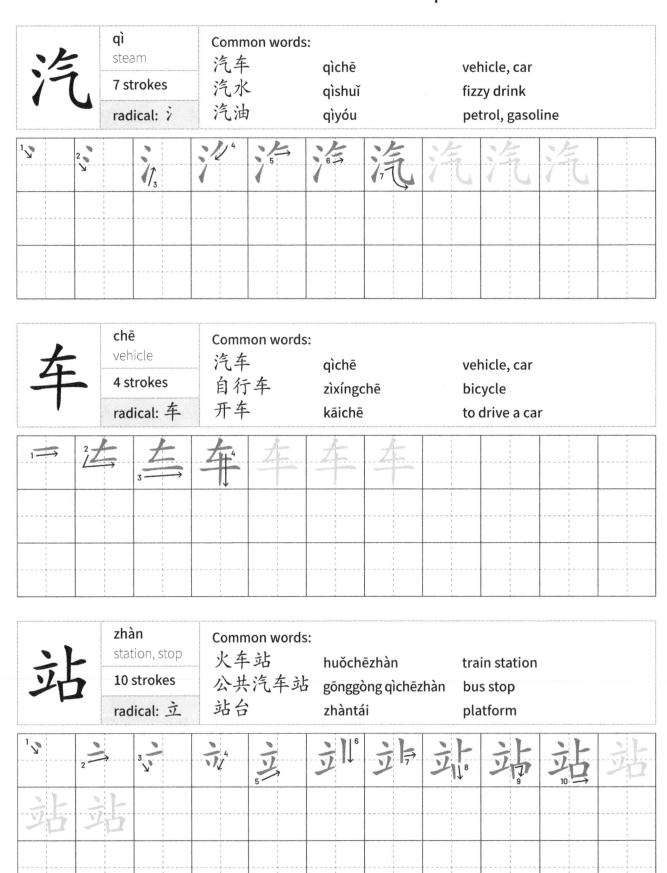

| 汽 | qì
steam

7 strokes

radical: 氵 | Common words:

汽车　　　　qìchē　　　　　　　vehicle, car
汽水　　　　qìshuǐ　　　　　　　fizzy drink
汽油　　　　qìyóu　　　　　　　petrol, gasoline |

| 车 | chē
vehicle

4 strokes

radical: 车 | Common words:

汽车　　　　qìchē　　　　　　　vehicle, car
自行车　　　zìxíngchē　　　　　bicycle
开车　　　　kāichē　　　　　　　to drive a car |

| 站 | zhàn
station, stop

10 strokes

radical: 立 | Common words:

火车站　　　huǒchēzhàn　　　　train station
公共汽车站　gōnggòng qìchēzhàn　bus stop
站台　　　　zhàntái　　　　　　platform |

机	jī machine	Common words:		
	6 strokes	飞机	fēijī	plane, aircraft
		机场	jīchǎng	airport
	radical: 木	机器	jīqì	machine

一 廾 才 木 初 机 机 机 机

手	shǒu hand	Common words:		
	4 strokes	手机	shǒujī	mobile phone
		手指	shǒuzhǐ	finger
	radical: 手	手球	shǒuqiú	handball

一 三 三 手 手 手 手

票	piào ticket	Common words:		
	11 strokes	车票	chēpiào	train ticket, bus ticket
		门票	ménpiào	entrance ticket
	radical: 西	彩票	cǎipiào	lottery ticket

一 亍 亍 西 西 覀 票 票 票 票 票

票 票 票

飞	fēi	Common words:		
	to fly	飞机	fēijī	plane, aircraft
	3 strokes	起飞	qǐfēi	to take off, to depart
	radical: 乙	飞行	fēixíng	flying

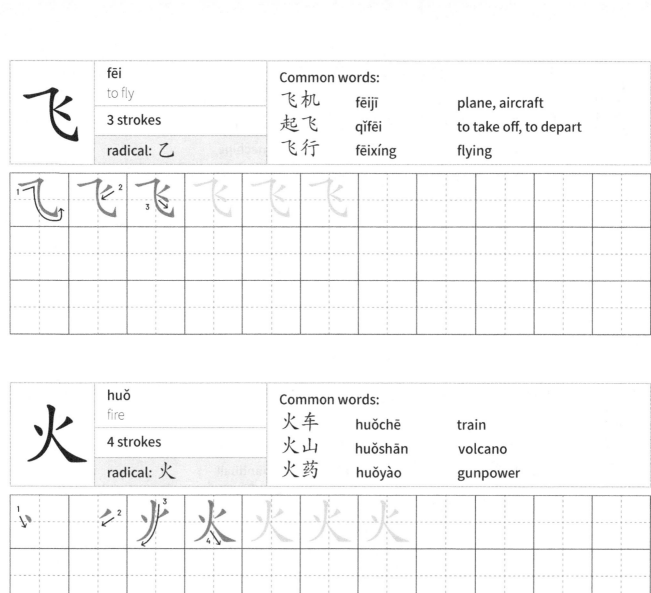

火	huǒ	Common words:		
	fire	火车	huǒchē	train
	4 strokes	火山	huǒshān	volcano
	radical: 火	火药	huǒyào	gunpower

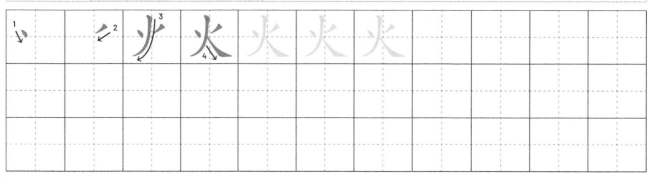

开	kāi	Common words:		
	to open, to turn on, to drive	开车	kāichē	to drive a car
	4 strokes	开会	kāihuì	to have a meeting
	radical: 一	开关	kāiguān	switch

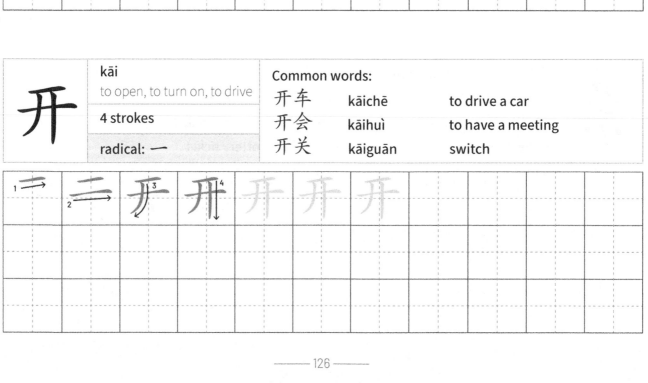

坐	zuò to sit 7 strokes radical: 土	Common words: 坐下　　　　　　zuò xià　　　　　　　　to sit down 坐飞机　　　　　zuò fēijī　　　　　　　　to take plane 坐公共汽车　　zuò gōnggòng qìchē　to take bus

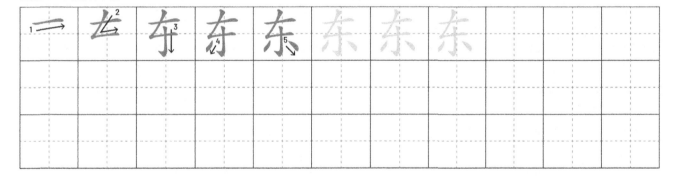

东	dōng east 5 strokes radical: 一	Common words: 东西　　　　　dōngxī　　　　east and west, thing, stuff 东南　　　　　dōngnán　　　southeast 东方　　　　　dōngfāng　　east

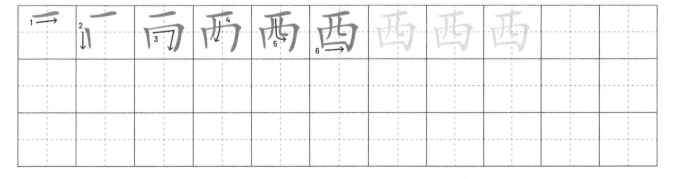

西	xī west 6 strokes radical: 西	Common words: 西方　　　　　xīfāng　　　west 西藏　　　　　Xīzàng　　　Tibet 西医　　　　　xīyī　　　　Western medicine

南	nán south	Common words:		
	9 strokes	南方	nánfāng	south
		东南亚	Dōngnányà	Southeast Asia
	radical: 十	南瓜	nánguā	pumpkin

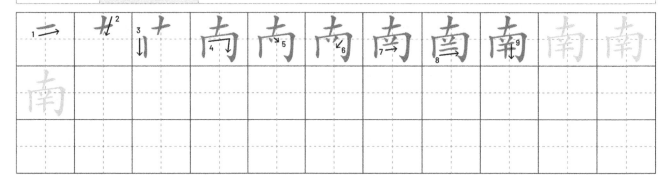

北	běi north	Common words:		
	5 strokes	北方	běifāng	north
		北京	Běijīng	Beijing
	radical: 匕	北极	běijí	North Pole

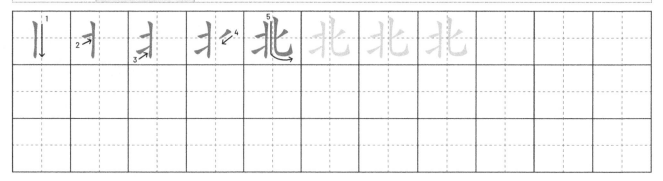

京	jīng capital	Common words:		
	8 strokes	北京	Běijīng	Beijing
		东京	Dōngjīng	Tokyo
	radical: 亠	南京	Nánjīng	Nanjing

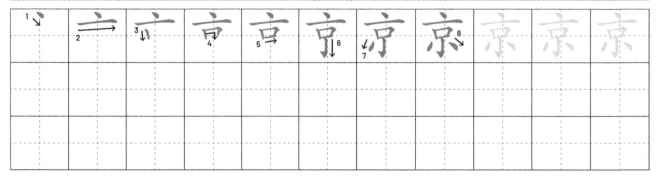

里	lǐ inside	Common words:		
	7 strokes	里面	lǐmiàn	inside
		房间里	fángjiān li	in the room
	radical: 里	里程	lǐchéng	mileage

里	曰	曰	旦	甲	里	里	里	里	里	

楼	lóu storied building	Common words:		
	13 strokes	楼房	lóufáng	storied building
		五楼	wǔ lóu	the fifth floor
	radical: 木	楼梯	lóutī	stairs

一	十	才	术	术	术	杧	枡	梻	楼	
楼	楼	楼	楼	楼						

路	lù road	Common words:		
	13 strokes	马路	mǎlù	road, street
		路上	lù shàng	on the road
	radical: 足	路人	lùrén	passerby

丨	口	吕	呈	足	呈	足	趴	趵	路	路
路	路	路	路	路						

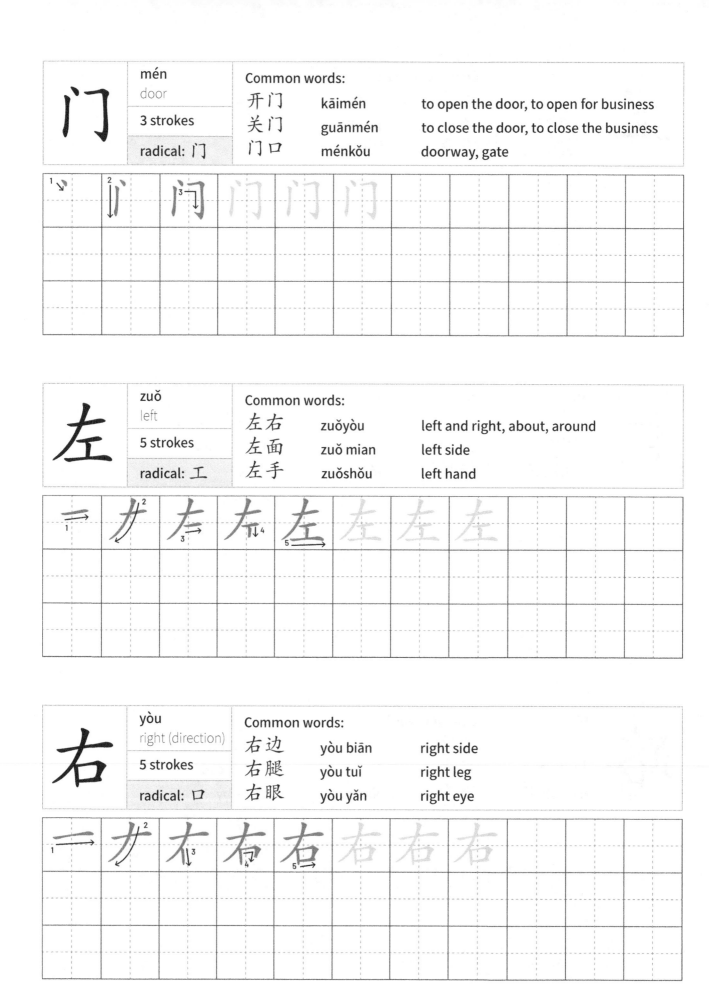

门	mén door	Common words:		
	3 strokes	开门	kāimén	to open the door, to open for business
	radical: 门	关门	guānmén	to close the door, to close the business
		门口	ménkǒu	doorway, gate

左	zuǒ left	Common words:		
	5 strokes	左右	zuǒyòu	left and right, about, around
	radical: 工	左面	zuǒ mian	left side
		左手	zuǒshǒu	left hand

右	yòu right (direction)	Common words:		
	5 strokes	右边	yòu biān	right side
	radical: 口	右腿	yòu tuǐ	right leg
		右眼	yòu yǎn	right eye

远	yuǎn far	**Common words:**		
	7 strokes	很远	hěn yuǎn	very far away
		远东	yuǎndōng	Far East
	radical: 辶	远方	yuǎnfāng	distance

边	biān side, border	**Common words:**		
	5 strokes	里边	lǐbian	inside
		外边	wàibian	outside
	radical: 辶	东边	dōngbian	east side

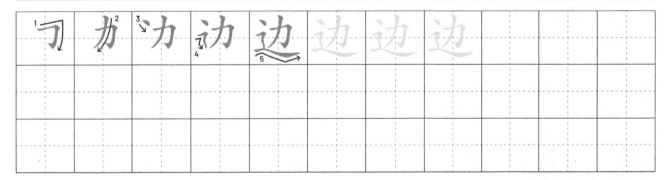

行	xíng okay, to walk	**Common words:**		
	6 strokes	不行	bùxíng	not ok, not work
		人行道	rénxíngdào	sidewalk
	radical: 彳	自行车	zìxíngchē	bicycle

WORD PRACTICE

汽车 **qìchē** vehicle, car

汽	车								

火车 **huǒchē** train

火	车								

飞机 **fēijī** airplane, aircraft

飞	机								

车站 **chēzhàn** station, stop

车	站								

车票 **chēpiào** ticket

车	票								

开车 **kāi chē** to drive a car

开	车								

坐车 **zuò chē** by car

坐	车							

东南 **dōngnán** southeast

东	南							

西北 **xīběi** northwest

西	北							

东西 **dōngxī** east and west, thing, stuff

东	西							

楼里 **lóuli** in the stored building

楼	里							

路上 **lù shàng** on the road

路	上							

左右 **zuǒyòu** left and right, about, around

左	右							

里边 **lǐ biān** inside

里边								

外边 **wài biān** outside

外边								

1. Write down the corresponding Chinese characters for the pinyin below.

(   )   (   )   (   )   (   )   (   )

    qì   chē   zhàn   jī   piào

(   )   (   )   (   )   (   )   (   )

    fēi   huǒ   kāi   dōng   xī

(   )   (   )   (   )   (   )   (   )

    nán   běi   lǐ   lóu   lù

(   )   (   )   (   )   (   )   (   )

    mén   zuǒ   yòu   yuǎn   zuò

(   )

    xíng

2. Please read the pinyin and write the correct Chinese characters to complete the sentence.

1) 我今天_____ (zuò chē) 上班。

   A. 坐车   B. 坐飞机   C. 汽车

2) 我想坐_____ (fēijī) 去中国。

   A. 车   B. 汽车   C. 飞机

3) 英国在中国的_____ (xīfāng)。

    A. 东方   **B.** 西方   **C.** 南方

4) 伦敦在英国的_____ (dōngnánfāng)。

    A. 东南方   **B.** 东北方   **C.** 南东方

5) 妈妈在我的_____ (zuǒfāng)。

    A. 上方   **B.** 右方   **C.** 左方

3. Look at the image below, then please write down all the corresponding directions in Chinese.

N _____.

E _____.

S _____.

W _____.

4. Translate the following sentences in Chinese characters.

1) Where is the train station?

_____

2) Can you drive a car?

_____

3) Now it's about 5pm in the afternoon.

_____

4) I would like to go by train to China.

_____

5) Beijing is in the north of China.

_____

5. Listening practice: Please listen to the audio and choose the sentences you have heard in each group.

1) A. 汽车站在北方。　　B. 车站在北方。　　C. 汽车站在南方。

2) A. 你会开车吗？　　B. 你会坐车吗？　　C. 你会开飞机吗？

3) A. 东西南北　　B. 东北西南　　C. 南北西东

4) A. 我家在六楼。　　B. 他家在五楼。　　C. 我家在五楼。

5) A. 伦敦在英国的东南方。　　B. 伦敦在英国的东方。　　C. 伦敦在英国的南方。

SEEING A DOCTOR! | 看医生！

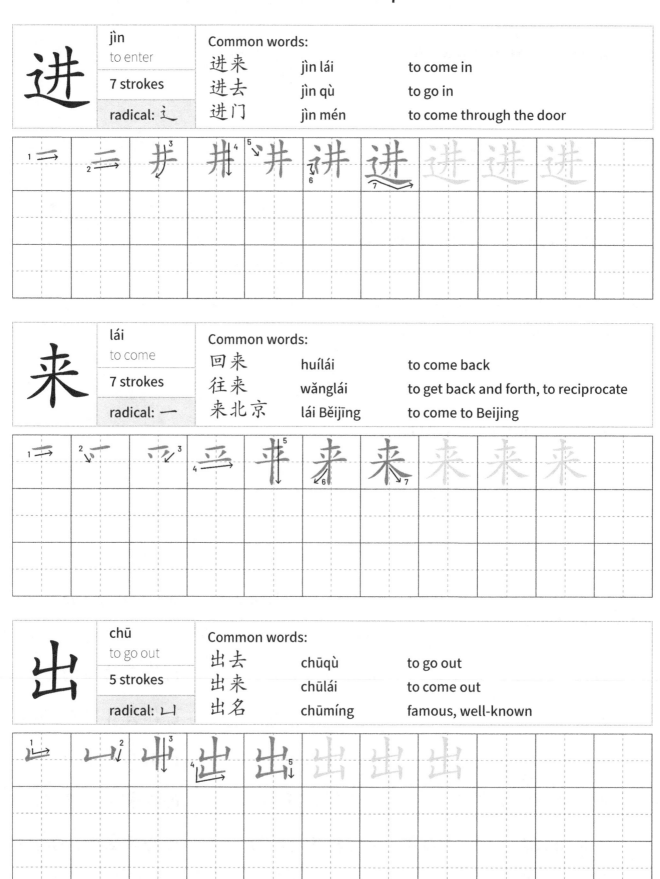

	jìn	Common words:		
进	to enter	进来	jìn lái	to come in
	7 strokes	进去	jìn qù	to go in
	radical: 辶	进门	jìn mén	to come through the door

	lái	Common words:		
来	to come	回来	huílái	to come back
	7 strokes	往来	wǎnglái	to get back and forth, to reciprocate
	radical: 一	来北京	lái Běijīng	to come to Beijing

	chū	Common words:		
出	to go out	出去	chūqù	to go out
	5 strokes	出来	chūlái	to come out
	radical: 凵	出名	chūmíng	famous, well-known

关	guān		Common words:		
	to shut, to close		关门	guānmén	to close door
	6 strokes		关电视	guān diànshì	to turn off the TV
	radical: ㇀		开关	kāiguān	switch

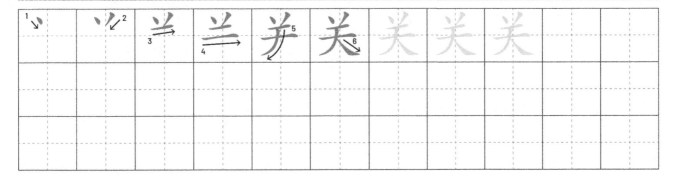

医	yī		Common words:		
	medicial, medicine		医生	yīshēng	medical doctor
	7 strokes		医院	yīyuàn	hospital
	radical: 匚		医学院	yīxuéyuàn	medical school

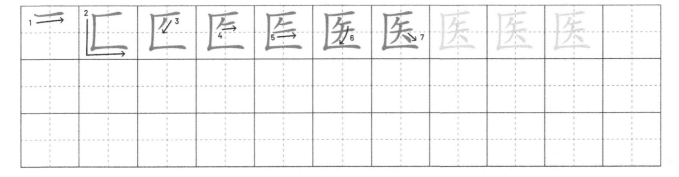

病	bìng		Common words:		
	illness		有病	yǒu bìng	illness
	10 strokes		看病	kàn bìng	to see a doctor
	radical: 疒		病人	bìngrén	patient

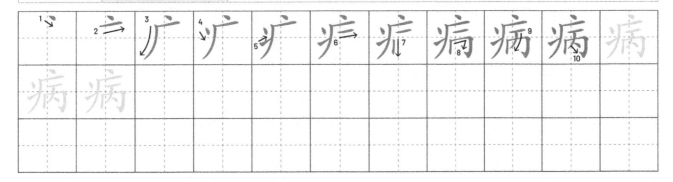

	lèi tired 11 strokes radical: 田	Common words: 很累 hěn lèi very tired 劳累 láolèi overworked 累积 lěijī to accumulate

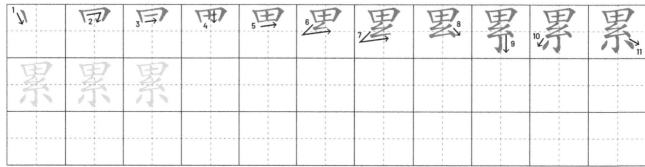

	shēn body 7 strokes radical: 身	Common words: 身体 shēntǐ body, health 身高 shēngāo height 身材 shēncái figure, stature

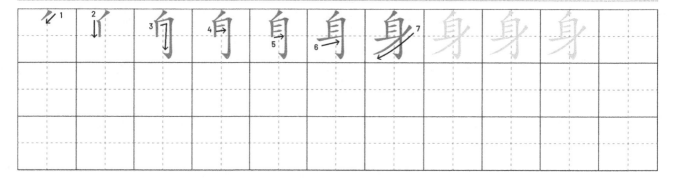

体	tǐ body 7 strokes radical: 亻	Common words: 身体 shēntǐ body 体育 tǐyù physical education, sports 体验 tǐyàn experience, to experience

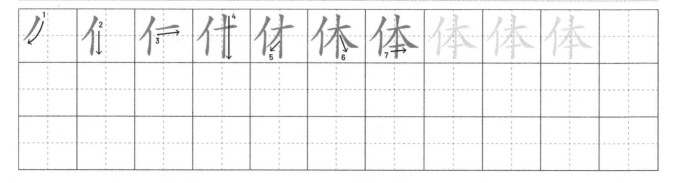

走	zǒu	Common words:		
	to walk	走路	zǒu lù	to walk
	7 strokes	走走	zǒu zǒu	to take a stroll
	radical: 走	走过	zǒu guò	to walk past

动	dòng	Common words:		
	to move	运动	yùndòng	movement, sport
	6 strokes	运动员	yùndòngyuán	athlete
	radical: 力	运动鞋	yùndòngxié	trainer

等	děng	Common words:		
	to wait	等候	děnghòu	to wait for
	12 strokes	等等	děngděng	to wait a minute
	radical: 竹	等于	děngyú	to equal to, to amount to

笑	xiào to laugh	**Common words:**		
	10 strokes	笑话	xiàohuà	joke
		笑脸	xiàoliǎn	smiling face
	radical: 竹	笑料	xiàoliào	laughing stock

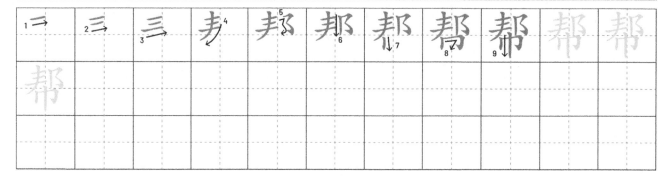

帮	bāng to help	**Common words:**		
	9 strokes	帮助	bāngzhù	to help
		帮忙	bāngmáng	to do a favor
	radical: 巾	帮手	bāngshǒu	helper, assistant

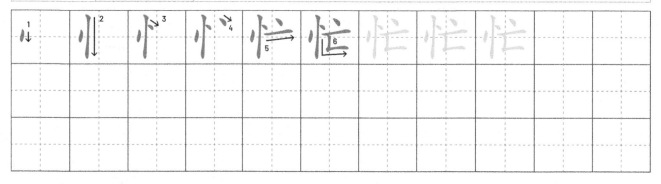

忙	máng busy	**Common words:**		
	6 strokes	很忙	hěn máng	very busy
		不忙	bù máng	not busy
	radical: 忄	忙碌	mánglù	busy, bustling

WORD PRACTICE

进来 **jìnlái** to come in, to enter

进	来							

出去 **chūqù** to go out

出	去							

关门 **guānmén** to close the door

关	门							

看病 **kànbìng** to see a doctor

看	病							

很累 **hěn lèi** very tired

很	累							

走路 **zǒulù** to walk

走	路							

运动 **yùndòng** movement, sport, to exercise

运	动							

等一等 **děng yī děng** to wait a minute

等	一	等						

帮忙 **bāngmáng** to help, to give a hand

帮	忙							

EXERCISE SET 13 练习13
SEEING A DOCTOR! 看医生！

1. Write down the corresponding Chinese characters for the pinyin below.

(   )   (   )   (   )   (   )   (   )

    jìn   lái   chū   guān   bìng

(   )   (   )   (   )   (   )   (   )

    lèi   shēn   tǐ   zǒu   dòng

(   )   (   )   (   )

    děng   xiào   bāng

2. Please read the pinyin and write the correct Chinese characters to complete the sentence.

1) 我今天_____ (qù kàn) 医生。

    A. 去看   B. 来看   C. 出看

2) 她昨天有_____ (bìng)。

    A. 饿   B. 病   C. 累

3) 爸爸的_____ (shēntǐ) 很好。

    A. 身休   B. 身材   C. 身体

4) 身体好要多_____ (zǒudòng)。

    A. 走走   B. 走到   C. 走动

5) 奶奶今天很_____ (lèi)。

    A. 累   B. 病   C. 饿

3. Translate the following sentences in Chinese characters.

1) Please come in!

_____

2) Please close the door!

_____

3) My older brother is very tired today. He is sick.

_____

4) His grandfather is ninety years old, and his health is very good.

_____

4. Listening practice: Please listen to the audio and choose the sentences you have heard in each group.

1) A. 等我！   B. 帮我！   C. 笑我！

2) A. 多走动很好。   B. 多走走很好。   C. 多走走不好。

3) A. 我奶奶今年的身   B. 我爷爷今年的身   C. 我妈妈今年的身
       体很好。   体很好。   体很好。

唱	chàng to sing	Common words:		
	11 strokes	唱歌	chànggē	to sing songs
	radical: 口	歌唱	gēchàng	to sing
		唱京剧	chàng jīngjù	to sing Beijing Opera

歌	gē song	Common words:		
	14 strokes	歌曲	gēqǔ	songs
	radical: 欠	儿歌	ér gē	nursery rhymes
		唱歌	chànggē	to sing songs

打	dǎ to hit	Common words:		
	5 strokes	打篮球	dǎ lánqiú	to play basketball
	radical: 扌	打人	dǎ rén	to hit somebody
		打针	dǎzhēn	to have an injection

球	qiú
	ball
	11 strokes
	radical: 王

Common words:

篮球	lánqiú	basketball
足球	zúqiú	football
地球	dìqiú	Planet Earth

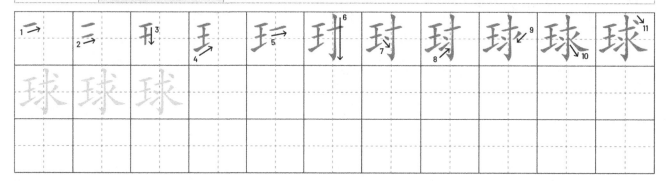

玩	wán
	to play, to have fun
	8 strokes
	radical: 王

Common words:

好玩儿	hǎowánr	fun
玩一会儿	wán yīhuìr	to play for a while
玩笑	wánxiào	joke

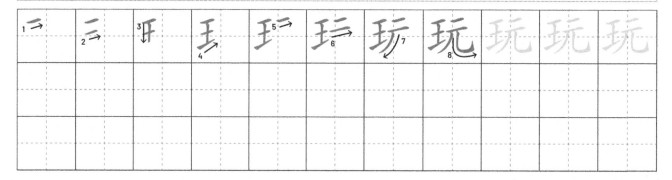

到	dào
	to arrive
	8 strokes
	radical: 刂

Common words:

来到	láidào	to arrive, to come
到达	dàodá	to arrive, to reach
到底	dàodǐ	after all

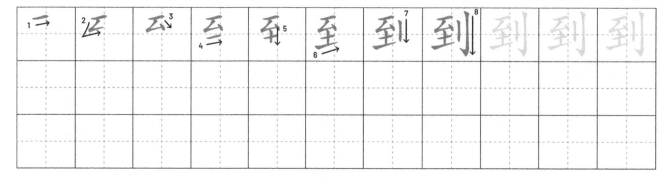

cháng	Common words:		
often	常常	chángcháng	often
11 strokes	平常	píngcháng	usually
radical: ⺌	家常	jiācháng	domestic trivia

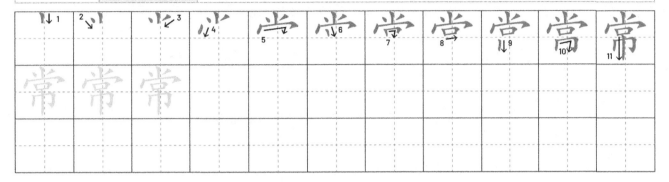

guò	Common words:		
to pass	过去	guòqù	to go over, past, previous
6 strokes	过年	guònián	to spend the New Year
radical: 辶	过桥	guòqiáo	to go over the bridge

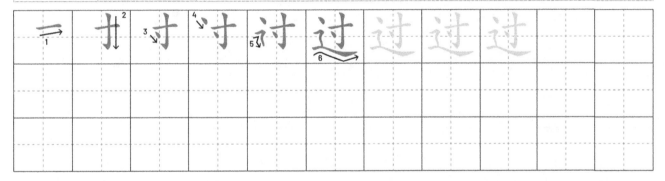

huí	Common words:		
to return	回家	huíjiā	to go back home
6 strokes	回来	huílái	to come back
radical: 囗	回去	huíqù	to go back

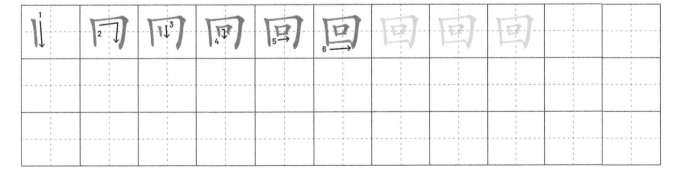

拿	ná	Common words:			
	to carry	拿住	ná zhù	to hold firmly
	10 strokes	拿着	ná zhe	to be holding of something
	radical: 手	捉拿	zhuōná	to arrest, to catch

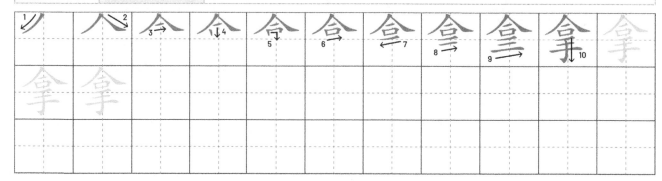

着	zhe, zhāo	Common words:		
	continued action or state	唱着	chàng zhe	singing
	11 strokes	喝着	hēzhe	drinking
	radical: 目	着急	zhāojí	in a hurry

住	zhù	Common words:		
	to live, to stay	住在	zhù zài	to live (in, on, at)
	7 strokes	住所	zhùsuǒ	residence
	radical: 亻	住家	zhù jiā	home

起	qǐ to rise	Common words:		
	10 strokes	起床	qǐchuáng	to get out of bed
		起来	qǐlái	to stand up
	radical: 走	看起来	kàn qǐlái	to look like, to appear

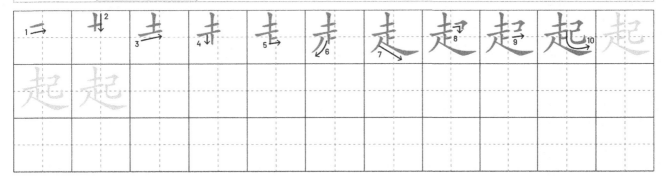

床	chuáng bed	Common words:		
	7 strokes	起床	qǐchuáng	to get up
		单人床	dānrénchuáng	single bed
	radical: 广	双人床	shuāngrénchuáng	double bed

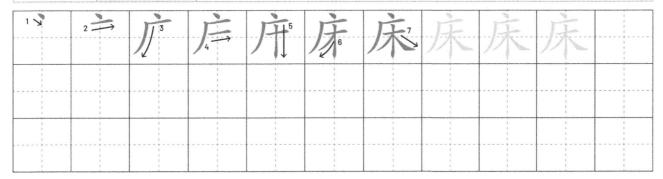

找	zhǎo to look for	Common words:		
	7 strokes	找人	zhǎo rén	to look for someone
		找东西	zhǎo dōng xi	to look for something
	radical: 扌	找零钱	zhǎo língqián	to give change

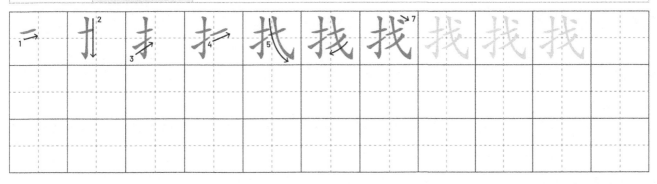

买	mǎi to buy	Common words:		
	6 strokes	买东西	mǎi dōngxi	to buy things
		买卖	mǎimài	to buy and sell, to do business
	radical: 一	买吃的	mǎi chī de	to buy food

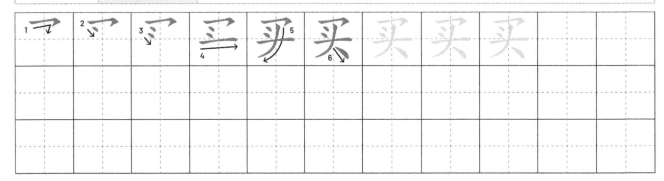

衣	yī clothes	Common words:		
	6 strokes	衣服	yīfu	clothes
		上衣	shàngyī	upper outer garment
	radical: 衣	大衣	dàyī	coat

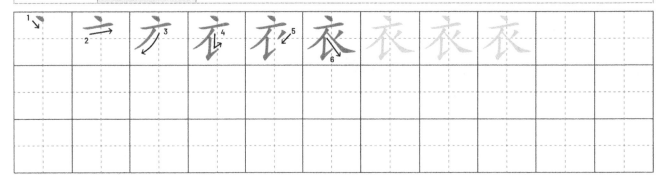

给	gěi to give, for, to	Common words:		
	9 strokes	给我	gěi wǒ	to give to me
		给钱	gěi qián	to give money
	radical: 纟	买给	mǎi gěi	to buy for

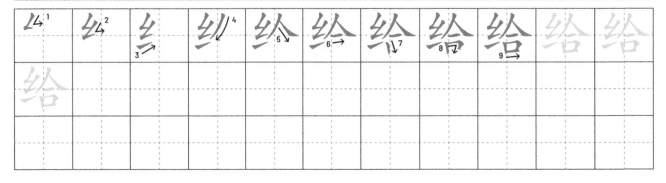

穿	chuān to wear, to put on	Common words:		
	9 strokes	穿着	chuān zhe	wearing
		穿衣服	chuān yī fu	to wear clothes
	radical: 穴	吃穿	chīchuān	food and clothing

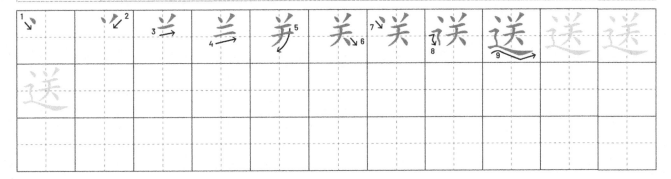

送	sòng to give as present, to carry	Common words:		
	9 strokes	送礼物	sòng lǐwù	to give presents
		送花	sòng huā	to send flowers
	radical: 辶	送钱	sòng qián	to give money

花	huā flower, to spend	Common words:		
	7 strokes	花朵	huāduǒ	flower, bloom
		鲜花	xiānhuā	fresh flowers
	radical: 艹	花钱	huāqián	to spend money

钱	qián money, cash	Common words:		
	10 strokes	金钱	jīnqián	cash, money
		给钱	gěi qián	to give money
	radical: 钅	价钱	jiàqián	price

元	yuán Chinese currency unit, element	Common words:		
	4 strokes	一元钱	yīyuánqián	one Yuan, equivalent of pound
		元素	yuánsù	element
	radical: 儿	单元	dānyuán	unit

角	jiǎo Chinese currency unit, angle	Common words:		
	7 strokes	一角钱	yījiǎoqián	one Jiao, equivalent of ten pennies
		角度	jiǎodù	angle, point of view
	radical: 角	拐角	guǎijiǎo	corner

睡	shuì to sleep, to go to bed	Common words:		
	13 strokes	睡觉	shuìjiào	to sleep, to go to bed
		睡眠	shuìmián	sleeping
	radical: 目	睡懒觉	shuì lǎnjiào	to have a sleep in

觉	jiào/jué sleep, to feel, to sense	Common words:		
	9 strokes	睡觉	shuìjiào	to sleep, to go to bed
		觉得	juéde	to feel, to think, to sense
	radical: 见	感觉	gǎnjué	to feel, to sense

WORD PRACTICE

唱歌 **chànggē** to sing songs

唱	歌								

常常 **chángcháng** often, usually

常	常								

拿着 **ná zhe** to be holding

拿	着							

住在 **zhù zài** to live in, at, on

住	在							

看起来 **kàn qǐlái** to look like

看	起	来						

找人 **zhǎo rén** to look for somebody

找	人							

买东西 **mǎi dōng xi** to shop for things

买	东	西							

起床 **qǐchuáng** to get up

起	床								

送花 **sòng huā** to give flowers

送	花								

一元钱 **yīyuánqián** one Yuan, equivalent of one pound

一	元	钱							

觉得 **jué de** to feel, to sense, to think

觉	得								

睡觉 **shuìjiào** to sleep, to go to bed

睡	觉								

1. Write down the corresponding Chinese characters for the pinyin below.

(   )   (   )   (   )   (   )   (   )

   chàng   gē   dǎ   dào   cháng

(   )   (   )   (   )   (   )   (   )

   guò   huí   ná   zhe   zhù

(   )   (   )   (   )   (   )   (   )

   máng   qǐ   zhǎo   mǎi   yī

(   )

   gěi

2. Please read the pinyin and write the correct Chinese characters to complete the sentence.

1) 我今天和我的朋友_____ (chànggē)。

   A. 打球   B. 唱歌   C. 进来

2) 她_____ (chángcháng) 看电影。

   A. 常常   B. 没有   C. 左右

3) 妈妈_____ (ná zhe) 一杯水。

   A. 坐着   B. 开着   C. 拿着

4) 我_____ (zhù) 在英国伦敦。

   A. 住   B. 走   C. 坐

5) 妹妹明天去买_____ (dōngxi)。

   A. 南北   B. 东西   C. 东南

3. Translate the following sentences in Chinese characters.

1) I would like to sing songs tomorrow.

_____

2) She returns home at 5pm every day.

_____

3) My family lives in China.

_____

4) It looks like tomorrow the weather will be very good.

_____

5) Dad is very busy today and tomorrow.

_____

4. Listening practice: Please listen to the audio and choose the sentences you have heard in each group.

1) A. 帮我拿着！   B. 帮我坐着！   c. 帮我看着！

2) A. 我常常买东西。   B. 我常常去买东西。   c. 我常常去买南北。

3) A. 妈妈给妹妹唱歌。   B. 妹妹给妈妈唱歌。   c. 妹妹给奶奶唱歌。

4) A. 妹妹现在住在中国。 B. 妹妹现在住中国。   c. 姐姐现在住在中国。

5) A. 今天看起来天气
      很好。   B. 今天看来天气
                        很好。   c. 明天看起来天气
                                            很好。

CONCLUSION

Now we have arrived at the end of this Chinese Characters Workbook. If you were a complete newbie before picking up this workbook, we hope you now come to the realization that Chinese character writing is very logical and completely doable. If you were someone who already knows how to write basic Chinese characters, we hope this workbook has expanded your vocabulary. If you were someone who aims to give the new HSK Level 1 exam a go, we are confident that by now you would feel well prepared for it.

We all know practice makes perfect. It is also true when it comes to Chinese character writing. Learning is a gradual process – you need to keep at it. Start with writing 3 characters a day and then gradually increase to 5, then to 10 characters a day, in this process you are cultivating the habit of writing Chinese characters daily without even knowing it.

Chinese is one of the hardest languages to learn and master, so be patient with yourself. Consistently be reminded of the 5 top tips of learning Chinese:

1. Concentration
2. Repetition
3. Association
4. Learn in context
5. Speak it!

We are happy to have helped you embark on the journey of writing Chinese characters. Hope you stay on this journey for many more years to come.

ANSWER KEYS

EXERCISE SET 1

1. 一, 二, 三, 四, 五, 六, 七, 八, 九, 十

 2. 11, 0, 21,84, 35, 76, 99, 0, 46, 52.

3. 零, 百, 三, 二十二, 半, 四十六, 七十八, 九, 十五, 五十七

4. 三十二, sānshíèr, thirty two; 六十八, liùshíbā, sixty eight;

   七十九, qīshíjiǔ, seventy nine; 十二, shíèr, twelve; 五十一, wǔshíyī, fifty one;

   四十四, sìshísì, forty four; 八十, bāshí, eighty; 十八, shíbā, eighteen;

   九十一, jiǔshíyī, ninety one; 二十三, èrshísān, twenty three.

EXERCISE SET 2

1. 我, 你, 您, 他, 她, 很, 好, 不, 们. 谢, 再, 见, 呢, 吗

2. 1) 你好吗? 我很好, 你呢?

   2) 他 (她) 们很好, 谢谢, 再见。

   3) 我们不好, 你们呢?

 3. 1) C

   2) B

   3) C

   4) C

   5) A

EXERCISE SET 3

1. 请, 问, 名, 字, 什, 么, 认, 识, 叫, 高, 兴

2. 请_问___, 高_兴__, __认__识, 什_么___, __名__字

3. 1) 你好吗?

   2) 你叫什么名字?

   3) 我很高兴认识你。

   4) 我不认识你。

161

4. 1) 请问, 你叫什么名字?

   2) 认识你很高兴。

   3) 我不认识你们。 Or 你们不认识我。 Or 我们不认识你。 Or 你不认识我们。

 5. 1) B

   2) A

   3) B

   4) A

EXERCISE SET 4

1. 是, 这, 那, 先, 生, 太, 小, 姐. 和. 中. 国, 人, 知. 道. 地. 方, 大, 哪

2. _先_ 生, 太_ 太, 小_姐__, 先生_和_太太, 中_国_人, __知__道, _地 方

3. 1) 这先生是中国人。

   2) 那小姐不是中国人。

   3) 你是中国什么地方人?

   4) 你知道中国吗?

4. 1) 我们是中国人。

   2) 她是小姐, 不是太太。 Or 她是太太, 不是小姐。

   3) 你是中国什么地方人?

   4) 她知道中国。

 5. 1) B

   2) C

   3) A

   4) B

EXERCISE SET 5

1. 日, 号, 星, 期, 年, 月, 天, 今, 明, 后, 昨, 前, 新, 去, 多, 少, 几, 岁

2. 1) 今天是星期一。

   2) 明天是八月七号。

   3) 昨天不是星期天。

   4) 新年好!

   5) 今天我十八岁。

3. 1) 八月十五号, 星期天or星期日 。八月十六号, 星 期一。

   2) 二零二零, 二零二二

   3) 九月九号, 星期一。九月六号, 星期五。

4. 1) 今天几号? 今天是八月十六号。

   2) 今天星期几? 今天星期一。

   3) 后天是星期三。

   4) 昨天是七月四号。

 5. 1) A

   2) B

   3) A

   4) C

EXERCISE SET 6

1. 早, 上, 晚, 下, 午, 时, 间, 白, 现, 在, 差, 分, 点, 两, 正, 候, 了

2. 1) B

   2) A

   3) C

3. 1) 现在是八点。

   2) 现在差十分五点。

   3) 现在八点四十五分。

   4) 现在四点十五分。

4. 1) 现在是下午两点。

   2) 现在几点了?

   3) 五点吗? 不是, 差十分五点。

   4) 现在是早上八点四十五分。

 5. 1) A

   2) C

   3) B

   4) A

EXERCISE SET 7

1. 文, 汉, 语, 外, 字, 学, 习, 读, 看, 书, 页, 说, 话, 听, 写, 错, 难, 真, 忘, 记, 会, 能, 用, 网, 对

2. 1) A

   2) B

   3) C

4) B

5) A

3. 1) 我学习汉语。

2) 她天天读中文书。

3) 我看汉语书。

4) 我早上说中文。

5) 学习中文很难。

6) 他忘记我的名字。

7) 我会说中文。

4. 1) 他会说外语。

2) 我会说中文。

3) 我天天晚上写汉字。

4). 他看(读)书。

5). 她早上听外语。

 5. 1) C

2) A

3) B

4) A

5) B

EXERCISE SET 8

1. 爱, 教, 班, 课, 本, 考, 试, 准, 备, 重, 要, 电, 脑, 影, 跑, 快, 慢, 放

2. 1) B

2) A

3) C

4) A

3. 1) 我爱学习中文。

2) 我今天晚上准备考试。

3) 学习外语重要。

4) 我用电脑上网。

5) 我明天晚上看电影。

6). 我慢跑。

4. 1) 我爱中文课。

   2) 他今天晚上看两本外语书。

   3) 我们准备中文考试。

   4) 我们星期六看中国电影。

   5) 我用电脑上网。

 5. 1) C

   2) B

   3) A

   4) A

EXERCISE SET 9

1. 家, 姐, 妹, 哥, 弟, 儿, 子, 口, 奶, 爷, 朋, 友, 有, 没, 和, 房, 干, 洗, 女

2. 1). A

   2). B

   3). C

   4). B

   5). A

3. 1) 我家有五口人, 妈妈, 爸爸, 哥哥, 弟弟和我。

   2) 她有一个男朋友。她的弟弟有一个女朋友。

   3) 我爷爷有三个儿子和两个女儿。

   4) 他的妹妹没有一个男朋友。

   5) 我家有三个房子。

 4. 1) C

   2) A

   3) C

   4) B

   5) B

EXERCISE SET 10

1. 吃, 饭, 菜, 饿, 渴, 喝, 水, 果, 想, 茶, 米, 面, 条, 肉, 包, 做, 鸡, 蛋, 坏, 块, 桌, 杯, 店

2. 1) A

   2) B

   3) C

   4) A

   5) B

3. 1) 我今天吃水果，喝茶。

   2) 她想明天吃面条。

   3) 我今天晚上做鸡蛋饭。

   4) 他不想吃米饭，他想吃鸡肉。

   5) 我想喝两杯中国茶。

 4. 1) A

   2) C

   3) A

   4) B

   5) C

EXERCISE SET 11

1. 气，冷，热，雨，怎，么，样，风，非，最，跟，从

2. 1) A

   2) B

   3) A

   4) B

3. 1) 大风

   2) 下雨

   3) 天气很热。

4. 1) 今天天气很好。

   2) 明天要(会)下雨。

   3) 昨天没有大风。

 5. 1) A

   2) C

   3) B

EXERCISE SET 12

1. 汽, 车, 站, 机, 票, 飞, 火, 开, 东, 西, 南, 北, 里, 楼, 路, 门, 左, 右, 远, 坐, 行

2. 1) A

   2) C

   3) B

   4) A

   5) C

3. 东, 南, 西, 北, 东北, 东南, 西北, 西南, 左, 右

4. 1) 火车站在哪儿?

   2) 你会开车吗?

   3) 现在是下午五点左右。

   4) 我想坐火车去中国。

   5) 北京在中国的北方。

 5. 1) A

   2) A

   3) A

   4) B

   5) A

EXERCISE SET 13

1. 进, 来, 出, 关, 病, 累, 身, 体, 走, 动, 等, 笑, 帮

2. 1) A

   2) B

   3) C

   4) C

   5) A

3. 1) 请进来!

   2) 请关门!

   3) 我哥哥今天很累。他病了。

   4) 他爷爷九十岁, 他的身体很好。

4. 1) B

    2) A

    3) C

EXERCISE SET 14

1. 唱, 歌, 打, 到, 常, 过, 回, 拿, 着, 住, 忙, 起, 找, 买, 衣, 给

2. 1) B

   2) A

   3) C

   4) A

   5) B

3. 1) 我想明天唱歌。

   2) 她天天下午五点回家。

   3) 我家人住在中国。

   4) 看起来明天天气会很好。

   5) 爸爸今天和明天很忙。

 4. 1) A

    2) B

    3) B

    4) A

    5) A

ENGLISH – CHINESE INDEX

A

to be born, person	生	shēng	32
bed	床	chuáng	151
before, front	前	qián	44
behind, back	后	hòu	44
below, to go down	下	xià	53
between, room	间	jiān	54
big, large, great	大	dà	36
book	书	shū	65
body	身	shēn	140
body	体	tǐ	140
both, all	都	dōu	70
business	商	shāng	108
brain	脑	nǎo	80
bright	明	míng	43
busy	忙	máng	142
buy	买	mǎi	152

C

call, shout	叫	jiào	24
can, meeting	会	huì	69
can, be able to	能	néng	69
capital	京	jīng	128
carry	拿	ná	150
center, middle	中	zhōng	34
character, word	字	zì	25

chicken, fowl	鸡	jī	106
Chinese	汉	hàn	62
Chinese currency unit, element	元	yuán	154
Chinese currency unit, angle	角	jiǎo	154
class, lesson	课	kè	77
clothes	衣	yī	152
cold	冷	lěng	115
come	来	lái	138
companion	朋	péng	92
continued action or state	着	zhe	150
country, nation	国	guó	34
courtyard, institution	院	yuàn	95
cure, treat	医	yī	139
current, present	现	xiàn	54

D

date, size	号	hào	41
day, sky	天	tiān	43
day	日	rì	41
difficult, hard	难	nán	67
direction, square	方	fāng	36
dish, meal	菜	cài	101
do	干	gàn	94
do	做	zuò	106

dot, o' clock	点	diǎn	56
door	门	mén	130
drink	喝	hē	102
dry	干	gān	94

E

enjoy, happy, happiness	喜	xǐ	64
east	东	dōng	127
eat	吃	chī	101
egg	蛋	dàn	106
eight	八	bā	12
electricity	电	diàn	80
enter	进	jìn	138
evening, late	晚	wǎn	52
exist, be, at, be alive	在	zài	55

F

face, surface, top	面	miàn	104
family, house	家	jiā	88
far	远	yuǎn	131
fast	快	kuài	82
father, dad	爸	bà	91
feel, sense	觉	jué	155
few	少	shǎo	46

flour	面	miàn	104
fire	火	huǒ	126
first, prior, former	先	xiān	32
five	五	wǔ	11
flower, to spend	花	huā	153
fly	飞	fēi	126
follow, go with	跟	gēn	118
food, meal	饭	fàn	101
foreign	外	wài	63
forget	忘	wàng	68
four	四	sì	11
friendly	友	yǒu	92
from, to follow	从	cóng	118
front, ahead, forward	前	qián	44
fruit	果	guǒ	103

G

get up, rise, begin	起	qǐ	151
girl, daughter, female, woman	女	nǚ	95
give, for, to	给	gěi	152
go, past	去	qù	45
go out	出	chū	138
give as present, carry	送	sòng	153
good	好	hǎo	19

grandma, milk, breast	奶	nǎi	90
grandpa, old gentleman	爷	yé	90

H

half	半	bàn	13
hand	手	shǒu	125
happy, pleased	欢	huān	64
have, has	有	yǒu	92
he	他	tā	18
heavy	重	zhòng	79
help	帮	bāng	142
high, tall	高	gāo	27
hit	打	dǎ	147
home, family	家	jiā	88
hot	热	rè	115
house	房	fáng	93
how, why	怎	zěn	116
how many, how much	几	jǐ	46
hundred	百	bǎi	13
hungry	饿	è	102

I

I, me	我	wǒ	17
illness	病	bìng	139
inside	里	lǐ	129

meal, cooked rice	饭	fàn	101
meat	肉	ròu	105
medical, medicine	医	yī	139
minute	分	fēn	55
money, cash	钱	qián	154
morning, early	早	zǎo	52
mood	兴	xìng	27
moon, month	月	yuè	42
most, the most	最	zuì	117
mother, mom	妈	mā	91
mouth, opening	口	kǒu	90
move	动	dòng	141

N

name	名	míng	25
new	新	xīn	45
net	网	wǎng	70
nine	九	jiǔ	12
no, not	不	bù	19
not	没	méi	93
noon	午	wǔ	53
north	北	běi	128
now	现	xiàn	54

O

often, ordinary	常	cháng	149
okay, to walk	行	xíng	131
old, outdated	老	lǎo	76
older brother	哥	gē	88
older sister	姐	jiě	33
one	一	yī	10
open, turn on, drive	开	kāi	126
other, another, do not	别	bié	118
out of order, bad	坏	huài	107

P

page	页	yè	65
pass	过	guò	149
period of time	期	qī	42
person, people	人	rén	34
person plural suffix	们	men	18
piece	块	kuài	107
place, let out	放	fàng	82
place of cultural activities, building	馆	guǎn	109
play, have fun	玩	wán	148
please, to invite	请	qǐng	24
practice, exercise	习	xí	63
prefix for ordinal number	第	dì	14
prepare	备	bèi	79

present	今	jīn	43

Q

question particle	吗	ma	21
question particle	呢	ne	21

R

rain	雨	yǔ	116
read	读	dú	64
recognize	认	rèn	26
remember, write down	记	jì	68
return	回	huí	149
rice	米	mǐ	104
right (direction)	右	yòu	130
rise	起	qǐ	151
road, path, way	道	dào	35
road	路	lù	129
run	跑	pǎo	81

S

see, meet	见	jiàn	20
see	视	shì	81
seven	七	qī	12
several, a few, almost	几	jǐ	46
shadow, film	影	yǐng	81

she	她	tā	18
shift, class	班	bān	77
shop, store	店	diàn	108
shut, close	关	guān	139
side, border	边	biān	131
sing	唱	chàng	147
sit	坐	zuò	127
six	六	liù	11
sleep, go to bed	睡	shuì	155
sleep, feel, sense	觉	jiào/jué	155
slow	慢	màn	82
small	小	xiǎo	33
son, child	儿	ér	89
son, person, seed	子	zi	89
song	歌	gē	147
south	南	nán	128
speak	说	shuō	66
station, stop	站	zhàn	124
star	星	xīng	41
steam	汽	qì	124
steam stuffed bun, bag	包	bāo	105
storied building	楼	lóu	129
study	学	xué	63

T

table	桌	zhuō	107
tea	茶	chá	104
teach	教	jiào	76
teacher, master	师	shī	77
ten	十	shí	13
test	考	kǎo	78
thank	谢	xiè	20
that	那	nà/nèi	31
think, would like	想	xiǎng	103
thirsty	渴	kě	102
this	这	zhè/zhèi	31
three	三	sān	10
ticket	票	piào	125
time	时	shí	53
time, to wait	侯	hòu	57
tired	累	lèi	140
too, extremely	太	tài	32
true, truly, real, really	真	zhēn	68
try, test	试	shì	78
two	二	èr	10
two	两	liǎng	56

U

use	用	yòng	69

V

vegetable, dish, food	菜	cài	101
vehicle	车	chē	124
very	很	hěn	19

W

wait	等	děng	141
walk	走	zǒu	141
want	要	yào	80
wash	洗	xǐ	94
water	水	shuǐ	103
west	西	xī	127
wear, put on	穿	chuān	153
white	白	bái	54
wind	风	fēng	117
words, speech	话	huà	66
what	什	shén	25
which	哪	nǎ/něi	36
which, what, how	那	nà	31
write	写	xiě	67
wrong	错	cuò	67

Y

year	年	nián	42
year(age)	岁	suì	46

Z

PINYIN INDEX

me	么	26
méi	没	93
mèi	妹	88
mén	门	130
men	们	18
miàn	面	104
mǐ	米	104
míng	明	43
míng	名	25

N

ná	拿	150
nǎ/něi	哪	36
nǎi	奶	90
nán	南	128
nán	难	67
nǎo	脑	80
mà/nèi	那	31
ne	呢	21
néng	能	69
nǐ	你	17
nián	年	42
nín	您	17
nǔ	女	95

P

pǎo	跑	81
péng	朋	92
piào	票	125

Q

qī	七	12
qī	期	42
qǐ	起	151
qì	气	115
qì	汽	124
qián	钱	154
qián	前	44
qǐng	请	24
qiú	球	148
qù	去	45

R

rè	热	115
rén	人	34
rèn	认	26
rì	日	41
ròu	肉	105

S

sān	三	10
shāng	商	108
shàng	上	52
shǎo	少	46
shēn	身	140
shēng	生	32
shén	什	25
shī	师	77
shí	十	13
shí	时	53
shí	识	26
shì	是	31
shì	视	81
shì	试	78
shǒu	手	125
shū	书	65
shuǐ	水	103
shuì	睡	155
shuō	说	66
sì	四	11
sòng	送	153
suì	岁	46

T

tā	他	18
tā	她	18
tài	太	32
tǐ	体	140
tiáo	条	105
tiān	天	43
tīng	听	66

W

wài	外	63
wán	玩	148
wǎn	晚	52
wǎng	网	70
wàng	忘	68
wén	文	62
wèn	问	24
wǒ	我	17
wǔ	午	53
wǔ	五	11

X

xī	西	127
xí	习	63
xǐ	洗	94

MORE BOOKS BY LINGO MASTERY

We are not done teaching you Chinese until you're fluent!

Here are some other titles you might find useful in your journey of mastering Chinese:

✓ Chinese Short Stories for Beginners

✓ Intermediate Chinese Short Stories

✓ 2000 Most Common Chinese Words in Context

✓ Conversational Chinese Dialogues

But we got many more!

Check out all of our titles at **www.LingoMastery.com/chinese**

Made in the USA
Las Vegas, NV
10 August 2023